Twelve Unlikely
HEROES

The Study Guide

Twelve Unlikely HEROES

The Study Guide

HOW GOD COMMISSIONED UNEXPECTED PEOPLE in the BIBLE and WHAT HE WANTS to DO with YOU

JOHN MACARTHUR

THOMAS NELSON
Since 1798

NASHVILLE DALLAS MEXICO CITY RIO DE JANEIRO

Published in Nashville, Tennessee, by Thomas Nelson. Thomas Nelson is a registered trademark of Thomas Nelson, Inc.

Thomas Nelson, Inc., titles may be purchased in bulk for educational, business, fund-raising, or sales promotional use. For information, please e-mail SpecialMarkets@ThomasNelson.com.

ISBN: 9781400204106

Printed in the United States of America

12 13 14 15 16 QG 6 5 4 3 2 1

CONTENTS

CONTENTS

ONE

ENOCH: THE MAN WHO WALKED WITH GOD

S OME HEROES ARE MADE IN A MOMENT. Others are defined by a lifetime. Though at times it appeared as if false teaching had swayed the entire Roman Empire, the fourth-century Christian leader Athanasius would not compromise. Enoch is rightly regarded as a hero for the same reason: he stood strong over a long period of time. The author of Hebrews summed up Enoch's legacy with these profound words, "He pleased God" (Hebrews 11:5). Amazingly, he "pleased God" not just for several decades, but for three hundred years!

REWIND

In all human history, there have only been two people who never experienced physical death. Both were prophets of God; both warned the wicked of coming judgment; and both lived at a time when following the Lord was utterly unpopular.

The biblical account regarding Enoch consists of just a handful of verses found in Genesis, Hebrews, and Jude (along with mentions of his name in 1 Chronicles 1:3 and Luke 3:37). Nonetheless, there is plenty of information given about him to include his amazing history in a book of heroes. Only eight verses in Scripture provide us with the details, but even with those limits, we encounter an individual whose life was both extraordinary and exemplary. As unique as Enoch was, he still sets a pattern for us of unwavering faith and uncompromising obedience.

What spiritual characteristics come to mind when you hear the phrase "uncompromising obedience"?

If only a few sentences were used to describe your character, what would be said?

In what areas of your life do you most often deal with the temptation to ignore God's ways in favor of your ways?

What do you expect God to show you in this lesson?

RETHINK

Enoch's world looked very different than ours does today. But the culture in which he lived was the same—characterized by comprehensive corruption, moral decay in every way possible, and open rebellion against God. The fact that people lived for so long was both a blessing and a curse. Those who sought to live godly lives in the pre-Flood era had to struggle against sin and endure its impact over many hundreds of years. That is what makes the examples of righteous men like Enoch so compelling: he stood against the corruption of his culture and walked with God for three centuries.

Enoch's faithfulness was an effective influence on his own family. That impact is especially evident in the life of his great-grandson Noah. Though Noah was born sixty-nine years after Enoch went to heaven, Enoch's testimony would have been passed down to him through his father and grandfather.

Based on your present rate and direction of spiritual development, would it be a blessing or a curse to live a long time? Why?

Your spiritual legacy will influence generations to come. What impact do you want to have on future generations?

What steps are you taking right now to develop the kind of character that will outlive you?

Twice in four verses Scripture says *Enoch walked with God*. In fact, that short phrase is all Genesis 5 tells us about the character of this man. But that's enough. Enoch lived in such a way that, after 365 years in this world, his life could be accurately summarized with repeated, sublime brevity.

What thoughts come to mind when you hear "Enoch walked with God"? Will a similar statement be made about you? Why or why not?

What can we learn practically about walking with God, so that we can follow Enoch's example? Scripture, where this theme is reiterated and expanded, reveals that walking with God includes at least three component parts. It begins with forgiveness from sin, consists of faith in the Lord, and results in fruits of righteousness. Understanding these three aspects opens up the door to the rich spiritual treasure that lies behind the simple words of Genesis 5.

REFLECT

In order for sinful people to commune with a holy God, they must first be reconciled to Him from their alienated sinful condition.

Enoch was a man who understood his own unworthiness and the need for a proper sacrifice. Enoch understood he was an undeserving sinner who needed a God-ordained substitute to bear the punishment in his place. Thus, his personal relationship with the Lord began when his sins were forgiven and he was covered by the righteousness of the Savior who would carry Enoch's sins to the cross and pay the penalty for them in full. Like all believers throughout every epoch of history, Enoch's testimony was one of salvation by grace through faith.

Describe your relationship with God. How did it begin?

Because of His infinite love, God is a lavish rewarder of those who put their faith in Him. As Paul told the Ephesians, "Blessed be the God and Father of our Lord Jesus Christ, who has blessed us with every spiritual blessing in the heavenly places in Christ" (Ephesians 1:3). He grants sinners forgiveness, clothes them in His righteousness, and creates in them a new heart. God turns former rebels into His children, giving them His Spirit, His blessings, and the promise of eternal life.

Enoch put his confidence in God's character and trusted God's will for his life. He obeyed God's commands and believed His promises. How does God's Word provide direction for your life?

Are you walking according to God's will? Explain your response.

One of the primary evidences of genuine salvation is a sincere desire, on the part of the converted, to know God intimately and obey Him fully. For this to happen, the believer must be purposeful and focused. This is an intentional and passionate pursuit. Like believers in Bible times, all Christians are called to walk in obedience, truth, and godliness. Of course, everything in society fights that effort. Secular culture is only getting worse; and the church, in many cases, has grown weak and shallow. The temptation to compromise and sin is immense and relentless.

How does your everyday life reflect the reality of your love for God?

What is your daily routine for growing in your knowledge and understanding of God and His Word? Is it producing the desired results? Why or why not?

REACT

Though we might not escape death in this life (unless we are alive when the Lord calls the church at the Rapture), we possess the same hope Enoch had. As those who have put our faith in Jesus Christ, walking with Him in full forgiveness and intimate fellowship, we can rest assured that we have received eternal life.

Review Enoch's life. How does your relationship with God compare to his?

What can you do this week to deepen your walk with the Lord?

What priorities need to be rearranged so you can better focus on your daily walk with God?

Enoch's walk with God did not end when he stepped into heaven. It became perfect! So will ours. For eternity, we will enjoy glorious fellowship with our Lord and Savior, as we worship and serve in the infinite wonder of His matchless presence.

TWO

JOSEPH: BECAUSE GOD MEANT IT FOR GOOD

JOSEPH'S STORY HAS BEEN RETOLD MANY TIMES and in many ways—from dramatic productions of technicolor dreamcoats to cartoon specials featuring talking vegetables. Spiritual lessons about brotherly love, moral purity, good stewardship, and patient perseverance have all been drawn from Joseph's life. Those are helpful lessons to learn, but they are not the reason that Joseph's experiences are recorded for us in the Bible. Until we see the big picture of what God was doing through Joseph, we will inevitably miss the profound and foundational truth the account of this unlikely hero teaches us.

REWIND

God had some practical life-lessons for Joseph and a plan for His chosen people—one that included sparing them from a severe seven-year famine, then bringing them to Egypt where, over the next four centuries, they would be transformed from a family into a nation to witness His glory. It was all part of God's plan to fulfill *bad things*

roll with it

Covid — 2 yrs
plans → Spring break
JOSEPH
→ serious of what
wanted to do

His covenant promises of a seed and salvation that would extend to *→ more research* the whole earth. *→*

As New Testament believers looking back on Joseph's example, we can see the principle of Romans 8:28 fleshed out in his life: "And we know that all things work together for good to those who love God, to those who are the called according to His purpose." As Joseph himself articulated, God intended the trials of his one life for the good of his people; and though Joseph did not suffer because God was punishing him for sin, he *did* suffer so that God could ultimately save sinners.

✱ Read Romans 8:28. How have some of the negative things in your life worked together for the glory of God?

Gold Seal - no job ⟹ this led to Seattle role
miscarriage ⟹ led to role in Hawaii for family support

✱ Why is it hard to see bad situations as ultimately being beneficial to yourself and others?

Painful, not easy

What does God want to do through your life to deliver hope to people who do not know Him?

What opportunities do you have because of the lessons you've learned through the struggles you have faced?

Burn out @ FCF — better prepared for OCC

RETHINK

The environment in which Joseph grew up was filled with family tension and strife. Conflict ran in the family. His father, Jacob, had tricked his own father, Isaac, in order to cheat his brother Esau out of the family birthright. Joseph's maternal grandfather, Laban, was also upset at Jacob for trying to sneak away from the homestead in Haran. His mother, Rachel, was in a constant jealousy war with her older sister, Leah. In a race to have more children, Leah and Rachel gave Jacob their handmaidens as concubines, which further complicated family relationships. When the family moved to Canaan, two of Joseph's half-brothers, Simeon and Levi, murdered an entire village to seek revenge for their sister, Dinah—causing deep distress for their father and strained relations with their new neighbors. Joseph's oldest brother, Reuben, even had an affair with one of his father's concubines, which Jacob later heard about. Needless to say, Joseph's home life was loaded with bad relations.

Describe your family relationships and three lessons you have learned through them.

Tri's Only Child -
I was raised with brothers & family that diloveryling together
Non Christian Mom elled—This

How does your past affect your ability to serve and honor God? Does it hinder your service or does it give you a platform from which to encourage others? Explain your response.

Understand Non Christian dynamic

Read Genesis 37:6–8. How would you respond to a
similar message from a close relative?

Joseph descended from being the favored son to being a kid-
napped slave. How did this fit with the dreams God had given him?
Without warning, he had become a victim of "human trafficking."
At seventeen, Joseph's whole world was flipped on its head.
Betrayed by his brothers, he had the joys of home and the security of
his father's love violently ripped away from him. Since we know the
end of the story, we also know that while the Lord never condones
evil, He does overrule it and accomplish His purpose out of it.

How is it possible for you to maintain hope in the midst
of circumstances you do not understand?

To know God has a plan
To see his faithfulness in past years
- Bad sales yrs
UC Berkley - UW

Joseph was purchased by Potiphar, a member of Pharaoh's court.
This opportunity allowed Joseph to be introduced to royalty and
the noble customs of Egypt. Such knowledge would later prove
essential. Joseph was also given a unique opportunity to develop
his leadership qualities. Joseph's placement in Potiphar's house also
ensured that, if he were ever found guilty of a crime, he would be
sent to the same place where Pharaoh's own prisoners were con-
fined. That, too, was part of God's divine plan.

REFLECT

Joseph eventually was accused of a crime he did not commit. But he was defenseless. It was his word against that of Potiphar's wife. When the master came home, it was Potiphar's slave and not Potiphar's wife who went to prison. Significantly, however, Joseph was not put to death for his alleged crimes. Normally in ancient Egypt, adultery was a capital offense. The fact that he was merely thrown in jail may indicate that even though Potiphar was angry, he knew Joseph's character and was not fully convinced of his wife's credibility. So Joseph was bound and taken captive again.

What steps are you taking to protect your character?

Don't put yourself in situations of compromise
- leave sales nights early   - act with integrity
- Areas of temptation.   - sales don't lie

If you were accused of a crime you did not commit, would your character prevent you from suffering the maximum punishment? Why or why not?

I think so - point to people & situations that support me

Joseph eventually had the opportunity to interpret some dreams. The Genesis account makes it clear that God was the one who gave the men their dreams and Joseph the interpretation. Like Daniel centuries later, Joseph knew that he had no ability to tell the future (Daniel 2:27–30). The Lord revealed the true interpretation, so that His power might be displayed and His purposes fulfilled. The time was coming when Pharaoh would need some-one who could interpret dreams. Right on cue, in the unfolding of this divinely ordained drama, the cupbearer would remember his extraordinary prison experience. God's plan for Joseph was coming together exactly as He intended.

> At this point in Joseph's life, he was in prison. Yet, God was at work in his circumstances. How have difficult situations and trials that you have experienced played a part in your understanding of God's plan for your life?
>
> *No job with Olly*

> If you had been in Joseph's situation, would you have maintained your confidence in God's plan? Why or why not?

Pharoah's dreams depicted a future reality—seven years of plenty followed by seven years of famine. If the Egyptians were to be ready for the coming catastrophe, they would have to begin storing up resources immediately. Moreover, a man with admin-istrative skill and managerial experience would be needed to organize the collection and storage effort. God had orchestrated Joseph's past experiences and trials for this moment. In a day, Joseph's fortunes had been completely reversed. That morning, he had awakened in his prison cell. By evening, he went to sleep in the palace.

How had Joseph's past experiences prepared him for his future role in the palace? We don't know how God will use our present circumstances to accomplish His purposes. But Joseph's example underscores the reality that we can trust God, no matter our situation. Do you find it easy or difficult to trust the Lord?

I find it easy now. Early in life harder
He has blessed & been so faithful.

What is your daily routine for growing in your knowledge and understanding of God and His Word? Is it producing the desired results? Why or why not?

devotional
prayer throughout day
reflection time

REACT

During the seven years of abundance Joseph was busy organizing the collection and storage of grain in all the cities throughout Egypt. His efforts were so successful that it became impossible to keep an accurate count of all the supply. It was also during this time that Joseph got married and started a family. When the good years ended and the famine began, Joseph's diligent preparations paid off. Not only were the Egyptians themselves spared from mass starvation, but multitudes of people suffering famine in the surrounding nations came to Egypt to buy food. Joseph's foresight and careful planning saved the lives of millions of people throughout the world. In an ironic turn of divine providence, Joseph's brothers came to Egypt in order to avoid death and were rescued by the very person they had sought to kill two decades earlier. Joseph was not interested in petty revenge. His trust in God's providential power outweighed any feelings of personal animosity toward his brothers. He recognized that everything that had happened to him was part of the Lord's perfect plan.

How did Joseph overcome his anger toward his brothers? What made it possible for him to forgive them?

Who in your life do you need to forgive? What keeps you from offering forgiveness?

Though Joseph's circumstances were unique to him, his perspective is one that all believers ought to emulate. The God who superintended the events of Genesis 37–50 still sits on the throne of the universe. He was sovereign over the circumstances of Joseph's life and He is sovereign over our circumstances too. We may not always understand what is happening around us, but, like Joseph, we can rest confident in the fact that the Lord is in complete control.

Pray for them specifically
Pray when they come to your mind
Text " " " " "
Check In
Not by themselves
Remind that live in world w/ Satan – Greater is the who is in me than the who is in
God inhabits praise – sing – music the world
Joseph story – maybe in pit today & in Pharoh's court tomorrow

THREE

MIRIAM: THE LEADING
LADY OF THE EXODUS

LMOST EVERYONE HAS HEARD THE STORY of Israel's
exodus from Egypt—when God miraculously liberated
His people from slavery. We all know about Moses, and
even his brother Aaron; and we are familiar with their respective
roles in that great deliverance. But how much do you know about
their older sister Miriam? The Bible depicts her as the leading lady
of the exodus. So, what was her involvement in the most important
redemptive event in Old Testament history?

REWIND

The Israelites lived in Egypt for 350 years before the exodus.
After Joseph died, the Hebrew people flourished and multiplied
greatly—going from a family of seventy to a small nation numbering in the hundreds of thousands. Over the years, the situation
drastically changed. In the centuries that followed Joseph's death,
"there arose a new king over Egypt, who did not know Joseph"
(Exodus 1:8).

The king's only concern regarding the Israelites was that their growing numbers posed a potential threat to his power. Thus, he told his people, "Look, the people of the children of Israel are more and mightier than we; come, let us deal shrewdly with them, lest they multiply, and it happen, in the event of war, that they also join our enemies and fight against us, and so go up out of the land" (Exodus 1:9–10). The Pharaoh conspired against the descendants of Judah, who suddenly found themselves enslaved in Egypt.

The descendants of Jacob cried out to God for deliverance. Among them was a man named Amram, the father of Miriam and her younger brother, Aaron. For Amram, Pharaoh's policy of murdering Hebrew babies was of great concern. His wife, Jochebed, was pregnant with their third child. If the baby was a boy, he was to be killed on the day he was born. That child was indeed a baby boy. And they named him Moses.

Miriam understood that the Egyptians would kill male Hebrew babies. Why was she willing to risk her life to save her brother Moses?

She heard her dad prayer for him and the way her mom spoke about him, She knew he was Special

What would you be willing to protect, even if it meant great personal sacrifice?

I would protect my children
I would protect Micah

RETHINK

Miriam had heard the prayers of her father, observed the affection of her mother toward Moses, and witnessed the faith of both in their protective defiance of Pharaoh's edict. Over the previous three months, she had naturally grown to love her baby brother and was burdened to help protect him in any way she could. It is likely that she even helped her mother construct the waterproof basket in which Moses set sail. And now she faced a great responsibility—to follow her baby brother as he floated in the Nile.

Miriam witnessed steadfast faith being modeled by her parents. Who are some examples of steadfast faith in your life? What have you learned by watching them?

> Ann Steffan -
> Mom & Dad - Faith - learned to trust & see
>   how faithful God is

Miriam's faith was characterized by taking action. What might have happened if Miriam had been unwilling to play an active part in protecting her brother?

> Princess might have found Moses but without being
> comforted might have given him away, Important
> that Miriam stepped in and brought mom.

Miriam's courage led to Moses' mother being paid to raise her own son! She could do so at home and without any fear of the Egyptian authorities. It is likely that Moses lived with his birth family until he was nine or ten years old, and maybe even until he was twelve. During those formative years, he would have been taught about the true God and about his forefathers, Abraham, Isaac, and Jacob. He would have identified with his people and learned that God had called him to be their deliverer.

> Miriam never envisioned everything that happened; she
> simply was willing to do what was right at the moment
> she had the opportunity. How do you know what's right?

In line with Bible, Holy Spirit, know

> How willing are you to take action when given the
> opportunity?

Sometimes!

At the beginning of Moses' life, the Lord used his older sister, Miriam, to watch over him and bring him safely back home. In her willingness to bravely approach Pharaoh's daughter, Miriam played a strategic role in her baby brother's return to his family. She was emboldened by the faith she had seen in her parents and which she herself possessed. Moreover, in watching the Lord rescue Moses from the Nile River, Miriam herself was being prepared for the day when she would see God deliver her people from their bondage in Egypt.

> Why is it so important for parents to take the lead in
> teaching their children about God?

Most influential, best time to learn is as a child

Child like faith key

What might have happened in Miriam's life if her parents
had left her spiritual development to others?

She wouldn't have been ready in time

REFLECT

The biblical narrative picks up the story when Moses was forty
years old. Having identified himself with his native people, Moses
"went out to his brethren and looked at their burdens. When he
saw an Egyptian beating a Hebrew . . . he killed the Egyptian
and hid him in the sand" (Exodus 2:11–12). The next day, Moses
discovered that others saw what happened. When Pharaoh heard
what Moses had done, the ruler sought to kill him. If the Egyptians
had already been suspicious of Moses, this event clearly confirmed
their worst fears. Running for his life, Moses fled to Midian—the
place where he would spend the next four decades of his life tending sheep and being humbled and shaped by God.

What did God teach Moses through his forty years of
exile? Have you ever experienced a time of significant
transition or extended hardship? What did God teach you
through that situation?

Humility. God humbles me whenever I get over confident

How did Miriam maintain her hope for a deliverer
throughout the forty years Moses was in Midian? Would
you have held on to hope for that long? Why or why not?

Would be hard — that's a long time

Miriam's excitement only grew when her brothers first confronted Pharaoh and then with each successive plague. Perhaps she remembered watching Moses float down the Nile, even as she witnessed the water of Egypt's mighty river turn to blood (Exodus 7:20–21). As frogs, flies, lice, boils, hail, and locusts afflicted the Egyptians, Miriam and her fellow Hebrews—protected by God in Goshen—must have been filled with awe and a growing realization that the Lord had finally heard their cries (Exodus 3:7), and their redemption from bondage was at hand. Eventually, the Hebrews received word that they would be allowed to leave Egypt. Their deliverance finally arrived.

The Israelites were redeemed from their physical bondage as slaves in Egypt. As Christians, we have been redeemed from our spiritual bondage as slaves to sin. In what ways is Israel's deliverance from Egypt a fitting picture of salvation from sin?

The mood of the Hebrews was dampened when they saw the Egyptian army approaching. Quickly their jubilation turned to complaints. They allowed their immediate circumstances to cloud their trust in God's power and deliverance. What situations in our lives can tempt us to doubt God's promises?

In the face of impossible circumstances, Moses trusted in the promises of the One who always does as He wills. His response to the people was charged with faith in the Lord: "Do not be afraid. Stand still, and see the salvation of the LORD, which He will accomplish for you today. For the Egyptians whom you see today, you shall see again no more forever. The LORD will fight for you, and you shall hold your peace" (Exodus 14:13–14).

How did Moses know God would deliver the Hebrews from the Egyptians? *Past Faithfulness Spoke to God*

Which of God's promises give you the most confidence each day? *Prob 3: 5-6*

REACT

As the Hebrew people crossed the Red Sea on dry land, Miriam must have felt a sense of awe. It was the brother she helped save who led the way. As they reached the other side, the people watched in amazement as the walls of water crashed together with a violence never occurring in any ordinary sea. In one catastrophic holocaust, the waters returned to their normal level to bury the mighty and massive army of Egypt like drowned rats. This was cause for worship and celebration. It is in the midst of this stunned, jubilant praise that Miriam appears! She, of course, had been there all along.

Read Exodus 15:20–21. What does this passage teach about Miriam's character and her relationship with God?

What are you doing now to create a lasting legacy of faithfulness to God?

Though they were not permitted to enter the Promised Land, these three siblings played an instrumental role in Israel's deliverance from Egypt—Moses as God's uniquely appointed deliverer, Aaron as Israel's first high priest, and Miriam as the leading lady of the exodus. Miriam's legacy is perhaps best seen in the fact that, in later generations, her name became one of the most popular for Jewish girls—especially during the time of Christ. In the New Testament there are at least six different women who bear the Greek form of her name ("Mariam" or "Maria"), which in English is translated as "Mary." These include Mary, the mother of Jesus; Mary Magdalene; Mary of Bethany, the sister of Martha and Lazarus; Mary, the mother of James and Joses; Mary, the mother of John Mark; and Mary of Rome (mentioned in Romans 16:6).

FOUR

GIDEON AND SAMSON: STORIES OF WEAKNESS AND STRENGTH

F OR US, THE WORD *JUDGE* IMMEDIATELY CONJURES up images of the courtroom. Whether it's the U.S. Supreme Court, with its nine distinguished justices, or any of the thousands of lower courts scattered across our country—a judge is a primary fixture on a bench with a highly defined jurisdiction within the American legal system. In our day, a judge wears a robe, wields a gavel, and presides over a court of law. The judge instructs juries, hears cases, and ensures that defendants receive the fair trial they've been promised by our nation's *Constitution*.

The Hebrew term, which can be rendered *judge*, also means *savior* or *deliverer*, and it is in that latter sense that the term applies to these unlikely heroes in Israel's history. They were both warriors and governors who sought to protect and assure freedom for their countrymen under the redemptive promises of God. For nearly 350 years in Israel's history, these saviors played a critical role in God's interaction with and protection of His chosen people.

REWIND

The book of Judges records centuries of Israel's repeated spiritual failure and God's continual grace toward His rebellious people. The old adage that history repeats itself is especially evident during this time in Israel's past—where a cycle of rebellion, punishment, and deliverance recurred at least seven different times. Over and over, Israel fell away from the Lord, and He punished them by allowing their enemies to oppress them. In desperation, the distraught Israelites would cry out to God for help, and He would graciously raise up a human judge to deliver His people (Judges 2:18). Then there would follow a time of peace—until a new generation forgot the Lord and the cycle was repeated.

During these four centuries, God appointed at least fourteen judges—at different times and in different regions. That appointment was not theirs by inheritance, popular vote, conquest, or manmade selection. Nor were the judges limited to a specific area or term. They were divinely random choices on the surface but sovereignly placed in God's chosen cause.

Why did God allow the Israelites' enemies to oppress them? Why did He later respond by raising up a human deliverer to rescue them?

Disobedience — worship idols.
Repent & need Judge to save them

When we persist in sinful disobedience, what should we expect from the Lord (see Hebrews 12:4–6)? How will He respond to us when we repent and ask for His forgiveness?

⟹ He loves you no matter what

RETHINK

The account of Gideon begins in Judges 6. From the outset, he is depicted as a man whose fear was greater than his faith. The same was true of his fellow countrymen. For seven years, they had lived in perpetual dread of the bordering Midianites and Amalekites, who repeatedly raided Israel's land, destroying their crops and stealing their livestock. Weary of hiding in caves in the mountains, the Israelites finally cried out to the Lord for help. When we first meet Gideon, he is hiding from the Midianites—attempting to covertly thresh wheat in a winepress (Judges 6:11).

> Though people today don't face the threat of Midianite invasion, many still live in fear and apprehension. What things tempt you to become fearful and to stop trusting the Lord?

Hardships, Financial

> How should you think about those things (cf. Philippians 4:6)?

Nothing to fear God will be faithful.

The Lord came to Gideon and instructed him to tear down an altar to Baal that was near his father's house. The young man obeyed, though with great trepidation. Again, courage was not a familiar virtue to Gideon. Nonetheless, he had shown a willingness to obey the Lord, and that was progress in his faith.

God has expressed His will for us in His Word, the Bible. Sometimes being obedient to His Word may require us to overcome our fears. What are some biblical commands that Christians find hard to obey due to their own apprehensions? (For example, the command to evangelize unbelievers sometimes instills fear in the hearts of believers.)

How can we overcome those fears?

God chose timid Gideon to lead an attack, so that His glorious power might be the only explanation for victory. Then God instructed Gideon to downsize the army! If Gideon had been nervous with an army of thirty-two thousand, imagine how he felt when twenty-two thousand of his troops left for home. Gideon would have been helped if he had remembered the words of Moses, who told the Israelites many years earlier, "When you go out to battle against your enemies, and see horses and chariots and people more numerous than you, do not be afraid of them; for the LORD your God is with you" (Deuteronomy 20:1). By reducing the size of the army, God made it certain that there would not be a conventional victory by the men of Israel.

God often reveals His power through our weaknesses.
In what areas of your life is God working to show His might?

— Communication

— temptation

— Work in Deals

In the thirteenth chapter of Judges, Samson's story begins much as Gideon's did. The Israelites were, once again, under the thumb of a foreign enemy: the Philistines. After years of oppression, the Angel of the Lord came to commission a new deliverer for His people. In this case, He presented Himself to Samson's parents, announcing to them that they would soon have a son who would one day be used by God to rescue the nation. Samson's father, Manoah, responded to the Angel's report in the same way Gideon had—by bringing a young goat and some grain as an offering to the Lord. Whereas Gideon was timid and fearful, Samson was brash and reckless. Gideon saw himself as weak and inadequate; Samson arrogantly believed himself to be invincible. Despite those stark contrasts, the Lord worked through both men to fulfill His sovereign purposes for Israel.

 Are you more like Samson or Gideon? What are the advantages of your personality? What are the dangers?

Gideon - think weak -
God revealed
reliance
when God comes thru to the credt

REFLECT

Read the account of Samson's life. Though he began with power and confidence, his end was tragic. The closing drama of Samson's life features a man who completely failed to advance from the reckless impulsiveness of his youth. The final chapter began when, as before, he fell for a Philistine woman. But even before he met Delilah, the text notes that he visited a prostitute in Gaza (Judges 16:1–3). While he was with her, the men of Gaza were informed and attempted to capture him. Escaping their effort, Samson uprooted the heavy city gates and carried them (bars and all) on his shoulders to the hills of Hebron, thirty-eight miles away! The sordid episode in Gaza highlighted both Samson's superhuman strength and his super-sinful weakness. His fatal attraction to pagan women was not only the pattern of his life, it proved to be the path to his death.

What habits in your life might negatively affect your usefulness to God?

- Pride   - lack of Humility
- Lack of faith

How did Samson's arrogance open the door to his ultimate failure?

Samson, so long blinded by might, arrogance, and lust, was eventually blinded by his captors, who gouged out his eyes and put him to work as a grinder in the prison at Gaza (Judges 16:21). The strongman who had triumphantly carried off the city gates was now utterly humiliated, a prisoner grinding grain with a hand mill in a dungeon. In this, the time of his most desperate weakness, the stage was set for the expression of his greatest strength and the most deadly act of his amazing life.

What do you think was the turning point in Samson's story?

Defeated by hair getting cut

What steps should believers take to protect themselves from moral failure?

- Vertical relationship
- Accountability

In terms of brute strength, Samson was the greatest champion in all of Israel's history. Yet he was also a man with horrendous faults. Even so, he is included—along with Gideon—in the list of those who walked by faith (Hebrews 11:32). His final act of valor shows that, in the humiliation and brokenness of his last days, he had come to truly depend on the Lord. He became a hero of faith by trusting God to use him in death and bring him into His presence.

REACT

Gideon and Samson represent opposite extremes. Yet both of their stories teach the same basic lesson—God's mighty power can override human weakness to accomplish His sovereign purposes. Gideon was a faint-hearted coward who, through the Lord's strength, delivered Israel by conquering the Midianites. Samson was an audacious strongman who, along with his superhuman strength, exhibited super-sinful weakness. Yet, the Lord graciously crushed and humbled him so he could be the divine weapon to accomplish victory for the Israelites over the Philistines.

Both of these men are presented as examples of faith in the New Testament. Their legacies might best be summarized by the phrase in Hebrews 11:34, "out of weakness [they] were made strong." It was in their moments of greatest frailty, when they were most dependent on the Lord through faith, that they were the strongest, because that was when God's power was displayed through them. Their heroism in the redemptive purposes of God was inseparably tied to their humiliation.

Read 2 Corinthians 12:8–10. How does this passage relate to your everyday life?

What might God do through your life when it is completely submitted to Him and His Word?

FIVE

JONATHAN: THE MAN WHO WOULD (NOT) BE KING

E VER SINCE THE ISRAELITES PROMISED at Mount Sinai to serve and obey God (Exodus 19:5–8), the nation had functioned as a *theocracy*. The Lord was the only King in Israel; He governed through the complex of judges, prophets, and priests whom He appointed to represent Him among His people. When the Israelites asked Samuel for a human king, they were simply articulating their discontent with the rule of God. They no longer wanted the theocracy—but rather a *monarchy* like their foreign neighbors.

Samuel warned the people about the inevitable downside of having a monarch. Kings forced their populace to labor in their fields and to fashion their military equipment; they drafted sons into their armies and took daughters captive to work as perfumers, cooks, and bakers in their royal service. For their own purposes, kings seized land, forced payment of taxes and tribute, took possessions at will, and made subjects, servants, and slaves of the populace. In all of these ways, the people would forfeit their freedom and even be abused. Samuel's final words of warning were the most frightening of all: "And you will cry out in that day because of your king whom you have chosen for yourselves, and the LORD will not hear you in that day" (1 Samuel 8:18). Once they set up earthly kings in power to replace the true King, there would be no turning back. The monarchy would bring disaster and even divine judgment.

REWIND

Tall, handsome, and from the warrior-tribe of Benjamin, Saul was the ideal candidate for Israel's first monarch—judging by external appearances. In reality, his physical attributes merely hid tragic weakness of character that was below the surface to start with, but would be unmistakably revealed during his long tenure as king. According to Acts 13:21, Saul reigned over Israel for forty years; his shortcomings surfaced almost immediately. Aware of his father's weaknesses, and familiar with his former role as a farmer, Jonathan was not intimidated when Saul became king. In fact, he did not hesitate to defy his father's authority when Israel's new monarch acted in utterly irrational ways. The conflict with the Philistines gave Jonathan the opportunity to demonstrate his military prowess. The conflict escalated into full-scale war, giving opportunity for Jonathan to prove himself a more courageous and capable leader than his apprehensive father.

What opportunities do you have to demonstrate your character and confidence in God?

— In front of kids — life choices

— " " " workers — work life — response to circumstances

— " " " friends —   *" " "*

What weaknesses do you have that might hinder your ability to be a spiritual leader? What are you doing to overcome those weaknesses?

fear - reverge love of God - casts out fear

- continuous time with God.

RETHINK

Saul's disobedience to God eventually cost him his opportunity to lead. Saul tried to explain away his sin. When faced with the just accusation of his guilt, Adam had tried to shift the blame. Saul employed that same time-honored "blame-someone-else" strategy with equally disastrous results. He pinned the culpability on everyone but himself—on Samuel for his late arrival; on his troops for their cowardice; and on the Philistines for the ominous threat they represented (1 Samuel 13:11–12). In reality, however, his blame shifting only intensified his sin.

How do you feel when you are blamed for something you did not do?

Upset - Not Fair

Why was it hard for Saul to take responsibility for his sin? Do you have the same problem?

He was King - he couldn't do wrong

Easier to blame others - makes you look better

By foolishly offering sacrifices to the Lord, Saul had violated the sanctity and uniqueness of the priestly office. He also failed to trust the word of God through Samuel. And the consequences were severe. Saul's faithlessness, however, was in bold contrast to the faith of his son, Jonathan. With the Philistine army still encamped nearby, waiting to attack, the young prince took his armor bearer on a dangerous covert mission (1 Samuel 14:1).

The Lord responded to the faith and courage of Jonathan by sending the enemy into full retreat, thereby delivering the out-matched Israelites from death and defeat. Jonathan's theology had motivated his battlefield heroics—the Lord was able to deliver with many or with few. Knowing God desired the destruction of His enemies and confident in His power, Jonathan put faith into action. While Saul sat under a pomegranate tree fretting about what to do next, his daring son once again took the initiative and saw the mighty power of God unleashed in victory.

When there is a spiritual battle, are you more like Jonathan or Saul? Explain your response.

Sometimes I feel more like Soul - Not taking action. But often-times I'm quick to act - Pray - go where the need is

What victories has God brought into your life? Where should you place your hope and faith when you face challenging circumstances?

-kids
- wife
- life
- work
- finances
- parents
-

faith + hope is in God

Back before the battle began, Saul's troops had been abandoning him in droves. Their defection, in part, had motivated Saul to disobey God by offering sacrifices before Samuel arrived. It may also explain the petty curse that the desperate king placed on his own men. In an apparent attempt to keep his remaining forces from desertion, Saul overreacted and placed them under a deadly oath: "Cursed is the man who eats any food until evening, before I have taken vengeance on my enemies" (1 Samuel 14:24). His soldiers were thus bound to win the victory before they could even eat their next meal!

Jonathan and his armor bearer had already left on their covert mission when Saul charged his troops with his unreasonable oath, so the prince was unaware of his father's foolishness. Later that day, however, when the Israelites were chasing fleeing Philistines through a wooded area, Jonathan found honey on the ground, stopped and ate some. Only in that moment, when Jonathan unwittingly violated his father's curse, did his fellow soldiers inform him of it. When Saul learned that Jonathan had violated his ridiculous oath, he determined to maintain his puny pride by putting his son to death. After all, everyone knew the king had rashly vowed to kill the guilty party, no matter who it might be.

What caused Saul to behave so irrationally?

Self-centered, Prideful, not right minded

What do his actions say about his relationship with God?

Did not have one,
Felt God was against him

REFLECT

By failing to trust the Lord and by offering sacrifices before Samuel arrived, Saul proved to be an incompetent leader who left behind a royal mess. He only accelerated his self-destruction as his reign continued. When God commanded him to completely destroy the Amalekites, including all their livestock, Saul again disobeyed. He left the captured king Agag alive and allowed Israel's troops to take the best of the sheep and oxen. The foolish monarch continued to rebel against God.

> Saul had specific instructions from God. We also have specific instructions from God, which are found in His Word, the Bible. Saul's example teaches us that incomplete obedience to the Word of God is really disobedience.
> In what ways are you tempted not to obey God's Word completely?

fear of future & finances
believing I am his child
discipleship & sharing faith

While Samuel was still grieving over the tragedy of Saul, God instructed him to anoint a replacement from another family to be king in Israel. Unlike Saul, who was physically impressive, the Lord chose an unimpressive shepherd boy. As a preteen youth, the youngest of eight brothers, David wasn't the tallest or strongest. But as the Lord reminded Samuel, "God sees not as man sees, for man looks at the outward appearance, but the LORD looks at the heart" (1 Samuel 16:7 NASB).

Then, when Saul was still alive and on his tarnished throne, David's royal training began. When an evil spirit terrorized the king, David—already known as a gifted musician—was selected to play the harp for him. Still living in Bethlehem, David went to the palace and was given an invaluable introduction to the royal court. When the Philistine giant Goliath threatened the Israelites, the Lord used this young shepherd to kill him with a slingshot, cut off his head, and secure the victory (1 Samuel 17:50). Like Jonathan, David knew that the Lord could save Israel using either many or only a few. No doubt, Jonathan was there when David defeated the colossus under God's power and must have recognized the kindred spirit of one whose faith was in the Lord in the face of deadly enemies.

God sees the heart, not the external person. Are you working more on developing your physical attributes or your spiritual attributes? What is your workout regimen for spiritual development?

Daily devotion, Daily reading, Continuous Communication

Sparked by the incident with Goliath, a deep friendship developed between Jonathan and David. First Samuel 18:1 describes the loyalty and devotion that characterized their unusual friendship: "The soul of Jonathan was knit to the soul of David, and Jonathan loved him as his own soul." The name *Jonathan* means "gift from the Lord," and the prince would certainly prove himself to be that for David.

REACT

Jonathan willingly gave up his own claim to the throne because he understood that the Lord had chosen David instead of him. And he had no resentment, only affection for the one who would reign in his place. Ironically, while Saul tenaciously (and futilely) tried to retain the throne for his son, his son happily offered it to the man he knew was God's choice to be Israel's ruler.

Jonathan's character is evidenced most clearly in his attitude toward David. Without question, he was a mighty warrior, a noble prince, and a loyal friend. But it was his unwavering faith in the Lord's plan for him and his future that set him apart as an unlikely hero. Jonathan did not merely *accept* his non-kingly role, he *embraced* it wholeheartedly—eagerly protecting and promoting the one whom God had appointed to be king instead of him.

Jonathan embraced God's plan for his life. He did not respond by becoming jealous, complaining, or getting angry. How are you responding to your current circumstances and the position in life where God has placed you?

Comfort

In what ways are you supporting others who are engaged in serving God?

Encourage
Financial

JONAH: THE WORLD'S GREATEST FISH STORY

THE OPENING CHAPTER OF JONAH is set in the midst of an intense storm. Jonah 1:4 explains that "the LORD sent out a great wind on the sea," indicating that its cause was supernatural. The seasoned sailors with whom Jonah traveled—men who had traversed the waters of the Mediterranean their entire lives—had never encountered anything like it before. Undoubtedly, they had survived to tell tales of countless storms in their many voyages, but perhaps none was like this one. The biting wind seemed angry and vengeful as it slammed the helpless ship into massive barricades of oncoming surf. The tongue-and-groove planks that formed the hull began to splinter and pull apart under the overwhelming pressure. Wave after wave crashed down upon her decks. The white-knuckled crew, clinging on and fearing they would not survive, cried out in panicked desperation. This storm felt personal. Indeed, it was.

REWIND

While the Gentile sailors frantically scurried about, bailing water and tossing any unnecessary cargo overboard, a seemingly oblivious Hebrew prophet was sound asleep in the hold of the ship. The boat may have been tossing and turning, but incredibly Jonah was not. It was only the ship's captain waking him that brought Jonah to conscious awareness of the chaos and deadly danger of the storm.

Once awake, however, Jonah was quickly in the middle of the greatest danger. When the crew cast lots to find who was to blame for angering the gods, Jonah was singled out and his suspicions were confirmed—he was God's target in the tempest. This storm, in fact, had been sent by the Lord both to chastise him for his flagrant disobedience and to halt him from running farther away.

What happens when believers run away from God in disobedience? Have you ever tried to do that? What were the consequences in your life?

Told God never go to Texas → went to texas

How did Jonah's disobedience affect the other people in his life? In what ways does your disobedience impact those around you?

Consequences still exist

RETHINK

Jonah had his reasons for fleeing in the direction away from Nineveh. The Assyrian capital was situated along the Tigris River (in modern-day Iraq) and boasted a population of six hundred thousand—making it an exceptionally large metropolis for that time period. It had become the capital city of a pagan enemy nation and represented everything evil that the Israelites hated. Nineveh was as wicked as it was impressive. The Assyrians were a notoriously brutal and wicked people. Assyrian kings boasted of the horrific ways in which they massacred their enemies and mutilated their captives—from dismemberment to decapitation to burning prisoners alive to other indescribably gory forms of torture. They posed a clear and present danger to the national security of Israel.

Have you ever excused yourself from doing something you knew God wanted you to do? How so?

more bold in testimony

Was your disobedience caused more by your fear or by your desire for comfort and convenience? Explain your response.

Jonah's hatred of sinners, regardless of how he rationalized it, put him in a dangerous position. As a prophet of God, he surely knew his duty—but he would rather take the chastening of the Lord (seeing it as the lesser evil) than be instrumental in Gentile conversions. That is a bizarre perspective for a preacher! Perhaps he also thought that by going far enough away, in the opposite direction, he would no longer be available for the task, and God would have to find someone else to go to Nineveh. He could not have been more wrong.

> How do your preconceived prejudices affect your
> willingness to be used by God?

> What would you do if given an assignment similar to the
> one given to Jonah?

Tough situation – wouldn't want to go

Jonah's attempt to run from God did not end well for the recalcitrant missionary. Spiritual rebellion reaps what it sows as God reproves and corrects those whom He loves (Hebrews 12:6). In Jonah's case, that correction came swiftly and in dramatic fashion—as his Tarshish-bound vessel was suddenly engulfed by a furious storm.

God would have been pleased if the prophet had fallen to his knees in repentance and promised to head back to Nineveh. Such a response surely would have stopped the waves. Jonah, however, stubbornly demanded to be thrown into the sea. In effect, he was saying he would rather die than fulfill his mission to the Ninevites.

> Have you ever resisted repenting for a sin you committed
> against God? Explain your response.

Why were you determined not to repent?

REFLECT

Jonah's three-day stay inside a fish was an indescribable horror. Lodged in the cramped and clammy darkness, he was likely unable to move and barely able to breathe due to the suffocating stench. The gastric acids of the fish's stomach ate away at his skin, and the constant motion of the fish combined with the changing pressure of the ocean's depths must have been absolutely nauseating. In the midst of his misery, the humbled prophet cried out for deliverance.

Read Jonah 2. Describe a time when you cried out to God.

Right Job in Maryland

Three days later, a wet, disheveled, and slime-covered prophet collapsed with a stench onto the sandy beach. He had just been violently expelled from his gastric prison by a fish that had endured three days of indigestion so that the Lord could teach Jonah a lesson. But the rebel prophet had repented. When the word of the Lord came to Jonah a second time, he would be sure to obey. The Lord's compassion toward Jonah not only resulted in the prophet's rescue but also in his restoration to ministry usefulness. In Jonah 1:2, God had commissioned the prophet to go to Nineveh, but Jonah disobeyed. Two chapters (and several traumatic events) later, the Lord issued the same command again: "Arise, go to Nineveh, that great city, and preach to it the message that I tell you" (Jonah 3:2). This time Jonah fully submitted, traveling east to the Assyrian capital.

> In what ways was God's mercy demonstrated toward
> Jonah in giving him a second opportunity to obey? Are
> there areas in your life where obedience is needed?

> Write a prayer of repentance, confessing areas of persistent
> disobedience to the Lord and committing to obey in those
> areas.

Jonah's message was a threat: "Yet forty days, and Nineveh shall be overthrown!" (Jonah 3:4). What happened next was a far more extreme and amazing miracle than the supernatural storm and the prophet-swallowing fish had been. The text declares the miracle in a seriously understated way: "the people of Nineveh believed God" (Jonah 3:5). Those few words describe the largest-scale revival recorded in the Old Testament, as the entire population of Nineveh—numbering in the hundreds of thousands—repented and turned to the Lord.

REACT

Most missionaries would be extremely elated by such an overwhelming response to their message. Not Jonah. His attitude of prejudicial hatred toward the Assyrians was still firmly embedded. If the people of Nineveh repented, it meant they would not be judged.

In His infinite mercy and grace, the Lord can rescue any sinner, even one as wicked as the pagan king of a barbarian nation. Jonah recognized the magnitude of God's grace, which is why he initially ran in the opposite direction; he wanted nothing to do with divine pardon being extended to Israel's hostile enemies. Ironically, when Jonah himself was in trouble, he cried out for God's mercy. But when the Lord extended grace to others, Jonah was filled with resentment. When God's wrath was withheld from the Ninevites, the prophet's wrath was aroused.

> Jonah did what was right with a bad attitude. Describe a time when you have done the same thing. What do you think God's assessment is of wrong motives?

*All about the motives
could do wrong but if will right motives - better
than do right w/ wrong motives*

> Why was your attitude bad? What did God teach you through that experience?

Although we are not Old Testament prophets like Jonah was, we have been given a mission similar to his. As New Testament believers, our charge is to take the gospel to those who are lost, proclaiming to them the reality of coming judgment and the hope of salvation (cf. Matthew 28:18–20). When we resist this responsibility, whether out of fear, pride, or a preoccupation with trivial things, we fall into the same trap that Jonah did. But when we are faithful to obey the Lord in this way, we experience the wonderful blessing of being used by Him to further His kingdom. There is no greater joy than seeing sinners embrace the good news of salvation. As the apostle Paul told the Romans, quoting from Isaiah, "How beautiful are the feet of those who preach the gospel of peace, who bring glad tidings of good things!" (Romans 10:15).

SEVEN

ESTHER: FOR SUCH A TIME AS THIS

T HE BOOK THAT BEARS HER NAME was not written by Esther, but about her. Maybe the author the Holy Spirit used was her relative Mordecai, or Ezra, or Nehemiah, or another Jew dwelling in Persia. Whoever wrote this history possessed a detailed knowledge of Persian customs and history, as well as Jewish features including a strong sense of Jewish nationalism. All of that plays richly into the remarkable labyrinth of this story.

The book opens by describing the expansive kingdom of Ahasuerus, the grandson of Cyrus the Great (ca. 600–530 BC), the Persian ruler who allowed the Jews to return home after seventy years of captivity in Babylon (cf. Ezra 1:1–4). Though many Jews went back to Israel at that time, many remained settled and scattered throughout the Persian Empire.

REWIND

According to Esther 2:16, four years passed before Ahasuerus got around to selecting a new queen. Even with all the necessary preparations, a new queen could have easily been enthroned within two years. Why did it take Ahasuerus so long to select Vashti's replacement?

The answer is found in Persia's two-year, unsuccessful invasion of Greece, which historically fits right between Vashti's demotion (in 483 or 482 BC) and Esther's coronation (in 479 or 478). As noted earlier, Ahasuerus himself returned to Persia in 480, before the war was over. Frustrated by the situation in Greece, the king came back to his capital at Susa (or Shushan), only to face the reality that he had no queen. With the war effort going badly, Ahasuerus needed a distraction. Selecting a new queen was the perfect diversion.

It is at this point we are introduced to the two main people of the book of Esther—two Jewish cousins who were living in the city of Shushan. Mordecai was roughly fifteen years older than his cousin, an orphan named Esther. Because Esther's parents had died when she was very young, Mordecai had raised her as his own daughter (Esther 2:7).

Based on what you read about Mordecai, which of his character traits stand out?

Stands up to Haman

Why was it hard for Jewish people to live in the Persian Empire?

RETHINK

An obscure Jewish orphan girl was exalted to the highest position of any woman in the world at that time. Out of the twenty-five million women in the empire, it had come down to Esther being singled out by the king himself. This was clearly no coincidence. A Power infinitely greater than Ahasuerus was at work, providentially orchestrating His purposes through the emperor's affections.

> Describe a time when you saw God's providential hand at work through the circumstances in your life.
>
> God working through a deal
>
> UW Mtg w/ Cullen Olson —

What can we learn about the providence of God from the extraordinary nature of Esther's life circumstances?

One day, not long after Esther was crowned, her cousin Mordecai was sitting at the entrance to the palace. There he evidently overheard a plot to assassinate Ahasuerus. These royal officials likely guarded the king's private quarters and may have been angry because of loyalty to the recently disgraced Queen Vashti. They had the motive and only needed the opportunity to make an attempt on the emperor's life.

The fact that Mordecai had such inside access to the private places in the palace suggests that he held an official position of prominence in the imperial government. When he learned of the plot against the king, he reported it immediately.

What would you do if you overheard a plot similar to the plot Mordecai overheard?

Mordecai was a Jew. Why did he report the assassination plot against the Persian king?

Right thing to do

Mordecai's actions were written down in the royal records—which would be used in a future day as the basis of his being rewarded by the king. Like all ancient monarchs, Ahasuerus was careful to honor and reward those who demonstrated their loyalty to him. Thus it was required to keep a record of notable acts of valor and special service rendered to the Persian monarch.

Though we do not have a human king, we do serve the King of kings. What would God write in His record book regarding your loyalty to Him?

Hmmm ... loyal but times of failure

Would an assessment of your loyalty and faithfulness to Him be cause for celebration or punishment? Explain your response.

I hope celebration

REFLECT

In the third chapter of Esther we are introduced to the villain, Haman, a man whom the king had exalted above his other princes and royal officials. From his introduction on, we are reminded that Haman was an *Agagite*—a designation repeated throughout the book (3:1, 10; 8:3, 5; 9:24). That he was an Agagite is no small detail. It is the origin of Haman's deep resentment toward the Jews and his effort to eliminate them.

Haman sought the advice of Persian magicians and astrologers who cast lots to determine the optimum day on which to annihilate the Jewish people. He then went to the king and deceitfully misrepresented the Jews as a rebellious threat to the empire who needed to be eliminated. Haman proposed that all Jews living within the Persian Empire ought to be killed (including those who had returned to the land of Israel).

Haman's plot was his way to manipulate a situation to gain favor and to seek revenge. In what ways are people today tempted to do something similar?

How can Christians avoid the trap of that kind of deceptive scheming against others?

When he heard about the genocidal decree, Mordecai tore his clothes, dressed himself in rags, poured ashes on his head, and mourned publicly. He must have been a spectacle, sitting outside the king's gate and wailing loudly. Undoubtedly, Mordecai realized that his earlier actions—refusing to bow down before Haman—contributed to this extermination as an act of retaliation. Haman's vengeful plan for the mass murder of the entire Jewish population, however, went far beyond a simple payback for Mordecai's disrespect. This was a much bigger scheme that involved Satan himself.

Mordecai informed Esther of what Haman had succeeded in accomplishing and sent Hathach back to her with a copy of the royal decree. He also urged her to plead with the king on behalf of the lives of the Jews. Mordecai's plan for Esther's appeal sounded simple enough. But it was considerably more complicated. In Persia, no one, including the queen, could appear before the king without his express invitation.

The queen was afraid of her potentially violent and irrational husband. Mordecai was putting Esther in a position to disregard the law and approach the king uninvited. The fact that Ahasuerus had not called on her for thirty prior days only increased Esther's apprehensions. Had she fallen out of his favor, and had the affection that led him to choose her turned to indifference, such that he would show her no mercy?

Esther was willing to put her life on the line in order to save the Jewish people. For what or who would you put your life on the line?
- Family

How does your love for God influence your recognition of those things for which you are willing to fight?

✳ Are the things you are willing to fight for important to
God? How do you know? What can you do to develop a
biblical set of priorities?

REACT

The book of Esther might be compared to a chess match in which
God and Satan (working behind the scenes) moved real-life kings,
queens, and nobles. It looked as though Satan, using Haman,
might put God's plans in check. But the Lord—who has absolute
power over Satan—checkmated the devil's schemes by positioning
Mordecai and Esther to find favor with the king.

Queen Esther and Mordecai were the human instruments
God used to rescue His covenant people from total destruction.
Esther, who came from humble beginnings, was an orphan in a
foreign land hundreds of miles from Israel. As such, she truly was
an unlikely hero. The Lord's plans for her were astounding and
unimaginable as He placed her in a position of prominence to protect the Jews from evil intentions.

In spite of her upbringing, Esther became a powerful
instrument in the hand of God. What does that teach
us about the power and purposes of God? Are there any
limitations that He cannot overcome?

Read Romans 8:28–39. In what ways does the power of God, as described in that passage, encourage your heart?

The Lord is still on the throne of the universe, just as He was in Esther's day. He is absolutely sovereign over the governments and earthly rulers of the modern era. Though the news reports rarely mention His name, God is the unseen power behind it all, perfectly orchestrating the details to accomplish His purposes. In the words of Psalm 103:19, "The LORD has established His throne in heaven, and His kingdom rules over all." What a comfort that is to all those who have put their trust in Him!

EIGHT

JOHN THE BAPTIST: THE TRUE MEANING OF GREATNESS

W HAT DOES GOD MEAN when He designates someone as *great*? In the thinking of popular culture,
greatness is usually defined in terms of privilege,
accomplishment, money, and power leading to some means of
fame. A truer view of greatness, albeit less popular, centers on
someone's lasting significance for providing far-reaching benefits
to people, not just personal celebrity status; it elevates those who
impact the world in significant and positive ways. But, whether we
measure greatness from the standpoint of popularity or from the
standpoint of human achievement, both definitions fall woefully
short of God's perspective.

REWIND

Before John the Baptist, there had been no prophet in Israel for
more than four centuries. Since the days of Malachi, no new word

of revelation had come from heaven. Nor had an angel appeared to men since the time of the prophet Zechariah, five hundred years earlier. But that long silence was about to be broken.

After recounting the incredible birth of John the Baptist, the biblical record quickly moves forward to the beginnings of his ministry. He lived much of his life in the obscurity of the Judean desert before the word of God came to him initiating his prophetic ministry when he was about thirty years old (Luke 3:2). At that time, he suddenly "appeared in the wilderness preaching a baptism of repentance for the forgiveness of sins" (Mark 1:4 NASB).

John was a contrast in every respect—from his prolonged isolation to his abrupt public appearance, from his rugged wilderness life to his dramatic preaching and baptizing ministry. He was born to a woman who could not have children. He came from a line of priests but ministered as a prophet. And he reached Jewish society by removing himself from it.

What was John the Baptist's message? Why was it needed after four hundred silent years?

John the Baptist pointed people to the Lord Jesus Christ. Why is that message still needed today?

RETHINK

Like the Old Testament prophets before him, everything about John's strange behavior was intended as an object lesson for God's chosen nation. He was not calling others to live or dress as he did, but he was calling people away from liturgically dressed hypocrites who were leading people to hell.

In the ancient near east, the coming of a monarch was usually preceded by the appearance of a herald who announced the king's imminent arrival and made final preparations for his stay. Along with the herald, a delegation of servants would be sent ahead of the royal caravan, in order to remove any obstacles in the road and make sure the way was ready for travel. Thus, the herald's responsibility was twofold: to proclaim the king's coming and prepare the way for his arrival. Those two components defined the privileged ministry of John the Baptist.

In what ways are you called to announce Jesus to the world?

What about your walk with God makes your message about Him believable? Are you a credible witness? Why or why not?

John's ministry is described as "the voice of one crying in the wilderness." To all who would listen, his thundering words reiterated one simple message: "Repent!" (Matthew 3:2). The Greek word for "repent" entails more than mere sorrow or regret. It means "to change the mind and will" and encompasses the idea of turning around and heading in the opposite direction. John declared that if the people would turn from their rebellious pride and embrace a life of wholehearted obedience, they would be ready for the Messiah.

John's message shocked the Jewish people because they assumed they were already included because they belonged to God's chosen nation. By ethnicity, they felt assured of a place in the kingdom of heaven, such that repentance was not necessary for them. On the other hand, the neighboring Gentile nations had no such privilege. John confronted that false notion head-on, boldly declaring, "Do not think to say to yourselves, 'We have Abraham as our father.' For I say to you that God is able to raise up children to Abraham from these stones" (Matthew 3:9). To the self-righteous Israelites who heard, John's point was unmistakably clear: they were in the exact same condition as the unbelieving Gentiles—spiritually dead, like stones. Unless they repented and were converted from sin to righteousness, they would not inherit eternal salvation. Instead, they would be judged. Being Jewish and religious, at that, counted for nothing before God but greater judgment.

In what ways do people today reflect the entitlement attitude of the Jews regarding their place in heaven?

If someone told you that he or she deserved to go to
heaven, how would you respond? How would verses like
Romans 3:23 and 6:23 affect your answer?

John knew his position and his task. Thus, he never sought honor
for himself but only for the One whose coming he proclaimed.
From childhood on, John had undoubtedly been told many times
of the angel's announcement of his birth and his calling—a purpose
he never compromised or manipulated for his own gain.

What are some practical ways that you can tell others
about Jesus? How are you supposed to make Him
known?

List the names of several people—family members,
friends, coworkers—with whom you would like to share
the good news of salvation. What steps are you going to
take to initiate those conversations?

REFLECT

As unthinkable as it was, Jesus came to John to be baptized. When
he first saw Jesus coming toward him, John declared, "Behold!

The Lamb of God who takes away the sin of the world! This is He of whom I said, 'After me comes a Man who is preferred before me, for He was before me'" (John 1:29–30). In that brief salutation, the baptizing prophet expressed the profound truth of Jesus' person and mission—noting both Christ's redemptive work as the Lamb of God and His eternality as the Son of God. Understandably, John's first reaction was that the Redeemer ought to baptize him and not the other way around.

John's baptism was a way for sinners to physically symbolize their repentance from sin. But Jesus came to be baptized even though He was absolutely sinless. Bewildered, John must have wondered, *Why would the perfect One who takes away the sins of the world want to participate in a ceremony that symbolizes a turning from sin?*

Why was John so reluctant to baptize Jesus?

The baptism of Jesus demonstrated three related things. First, it portrayed His willingness to identify with the sinners whom He came to save. As the first act of His public ministry, the Friend of Sinners associated Himself with those who were unrighteous—by submitting to a baptism designed for sinners. Second, His baptism served as a symbol of His death and resurrection. It prefigured the final act of His public ministry, His crucifixion and subsequent victory over death. Finally, Jesus' baptism served as a coronation ceremony and as a fitting beginning to His public work. When He came out of the water, God the Father commissioned Him with a voice from heaven.

Review each of the three statements above. What does each statement reveal about Jesus' character and purpose?

1.

2.

3.

REACT

From an earthly perspective, John's life and career ended in disaster. He had been a zealous, fearless prophet, faithfully fulfilling his role and boldly saying exactly what God called him to say. He was courageous and confrontational, but his unwavering commitment to the Lord landed him in prison. He eventually was beheaded.

From the world's point of view John achieved nothing of lasting value. Rather, he was hated, despised, and decapitated by his enemies. But in terms of divine approval and privilege, no one had ever been given a more noble calling than John.

It may be a shock to our superficial society to learn that true greatness is not defined in terms of human achievement, athletic prowess, financial gain, political power, or celebrity status. Instead, it is measured by how one relates to the person and work of Jesus Christ. John the Baptist was great because of his proximity to the Messiah. Similarly for us, true greatness is found in faithfully acknowledging the Savior. It is derived from our relationship to the One far greater than John—the Lord Jesus Christ.

What is your definition of greatness? How does it compare to the greatness demonstrated by John?

What are you doing in your life to become great in God's eyes? What priorities need to change (cf. 1 Peter 5:5–6)?

Upon arriving in heaven, our privilege will be elevated infinitely, as was John's. There, our faith will be sight, and our hope will be realized as we praise our Savior face-to-face. John's unique greatness was with regard to his role in human history. In terms of spiritual inheritance, however, even John's earthly greatness cannot compare to what he and every believer will enjoy in the glories of heaven.

One day we will meet John and for all of eternity join with him in worshipping the very Savior whose coming he so faithfully proclaimed: Jesus Christ, the Lamb of God, who takes away the sins of the world.

NINE

JAMES: THE BROTHER
OF OUR LORD

WHAT WOULD IT HAVE BEEN LIKE to live and grow up in the same family as Jesus? For His brothers and sisters, that question was not hypothetical. It was their daily reality. Jesus, of course, was not Joseph's biological son. So His siblings were technically His half-brothers and half-sisters. But clearly, because He lived with the family as the earthly son of both Mary and Joseph (Matthew 13:55; Luke 2:48) and as the older brother of His siblings, He was one of them. It was in that context that our Lord developed from boyhood into manhood. For roughly thirty years, He humbly worked as the son of a carpenter in the small village of Nazareth alongside His siblings.

REWIND

No indication is given in any of the four Gospels that Jesus' brothers came to believe in Him during the years of His public ministry. But, after His death, resurrection, and ascension, there is a dramatic and miraculous change. His brothers are present among the believers who have gathered in the Upper Room, awaiting the coming of the Spirit at Pentecost! According to Acts 1:14, after Jesus ascended to heaven, the apostles "continued with one accord in prayer and supplication, with the women and Mary the mother of Jesus, and with His brothers." James, Simon, Joses, and Jude, no longer antagonistic, had come to believe in Him as Messiah and Lord.

So James—the stubbornly skeptical second-born son of Mary—came all the way to saving faith in his older half-brother, the Lord Jesus Christ, through a post-resurrection appearance. Thus, James was there when the church was founded on the Day of Pentecost, and it would not be long before he would rise to a strategic leadership role. Jesus' other brothers, too, became instrumental members of the early church. Jude, for example, would write the New Testament epistle that bears his name.

Why was it hard for Jesus' siblings to believe He was the Messiah?

Grew up a normal kid - just sinless

What do you think happened that made Jesus' siblings believe in Him?

Seeing him after resurrection

What happened in your life to cause you to believe in Him?

Life - & seeing His influence & impact

RETHINK

The New Testament does not reveal much about the personal life of James. He was from Nazareth, of course. We can guess that, like Jesus, he was trained as a carpenter under the tutelage of his father, Joseph. As a Galilean, he not only spoke Aramaic but also Greek—which explains the excellent Greek found in his epistle. From Paul's statement in 1 Corinthians 9:5, we also learn that he was married.

Although he had known Jesus for more than three decades, he did not believe in Him until his risen brother graciously appeared to him and saved him. At the establishment of the church, James was poised for usefulness in ministry.

How has God uniquely gifted you for ministry and service?

In what ways are your gifts being used for His glory and honor?

In looking back over his life, it is difficult to overstate the strategic importance of James's influence. He led the infant church during a very tense and critical time. The church was newly born and emerging out of Judaism. Many Jewish Christians were still holding on to elements of their religious past such as going to the temple to participate in the ceremonies, festivals, and activities so familiar to them. But a shift toward freedom was slowly taking place. Moreover, believers were starting to reach Gentiles with the gospel. In so doing, they wanted to emphasize the liberty that exists in Christ, but without offending overly scrupulous Jews. It's little wonder that there was confusion surrounding the law during this period of transition from Israel to the church.

In many ways, James was the first model pastor. Unlike the twelve apostles, who eventually left Jerusalem to take the gospel throughout the world, James never left. He stayed with the church he loved, leading it faithfully for more than thirty years until the day he was killed. His commitment to the flock under his care never wavered. He was characterized by commitment to the truth but also by compassion for the consciences of his fellow Jews who were still sensitive to the traditions of Judaism. That he had a shepherd's heart is seen not only in how he cared for the church, but also in what he wrote—the epistle that bears his name.

What will be your spiritual legacy?
- kids
- churches - youth, men, small groups, elders

In what ways are you making a positive impact for the sake of the Lord Jesus on your church and community?

REFLECT

There are five things that stand out about James. First, James was a man of true humility. This is evident because, although he was the son of Mary, the half-brother of Jesus, and the leader of the Jerusalem church, he began his letter by describing himself simply as "a bondservant [literally, *slave*] of God and of the Lord Jesus Christ" (James 1:1). He made no mention of his familial relationships or of his prominent position in Jerusalem. Rather, he emphasized that he was the slave of God and of the Lord Jesus.

Second, James was a righteous man. In fact, he is known in church history as "James the Just." Appropriately, the theme of righteous living permeates his epistle. In just five chapters, he packed fifty imperatives—repeatedly commanding his readers to embrace a life of submissive obedience to God and His Word. His letter stresses the application of truth, emphasizing the spiritual fruit that should characterize the life of every true Christian. As a pastor, James had seen the devastating effects of pride, anger, selfishness, favoritism, materialism, and divisiveness within the church. He wrote to warn his readers to avoid those sin-laden traps.

Third, James was a loving pastor. He appears as a man of great compassion and sympathy, especially toward the poor and destitute. He showed no tolerance for favoritism in the church; instead, he encouraged unity within the body of Christ. The church, he wrote, ought to be a fellowship of rich and poor, in which the needs of each are met and communication is characterized by heavenly wisdom. There must be true oneness as believers submit to their elders and faithfully pray for one another. He saw the church as a group of people who ought to humbly love one another. He even referred to them as his "beloved."

Fourth, James was a man of the Word and prayer (cf. Acts 6:4). His mastery of Scripture is seen in the fact that his short letter contains four direct quotes from the Old Testament and more than forty Old Testament allusions. It also includes a number of parallels to the Sermon on the Mount, thereby echoing the teachings of Jesus. He urged his readers to listen to and obey the Word and not to be forgetful hearers.

Fifth, James was a theologian. In his one letter, he provided a theology of suffering; a theology of sin and temptation; a theology of fallenness; a theology of the demonic world; a theology of the law and faith; a theology of the church; and a theology of God and Christ. He presented Christ as the Source of wisdom; the One before whom all men and women are humbled; the One who controls all history and human destiny; the coming King; and the great Physician.

What might people say about your humility?

need some work

What might people say about your righteousness?

trying

What might people say about your self-sacrifice in ministry?

more so then than now

What might people say about your personal spiritual disciplines? *OK*

What might people say about your knowledge of God's Word? *Good*

In which areas are you the strongest?

In which areas are you the weakest? What is your plan for improving these areas?

In some ways, we might expect the half-brother of Jesus to be an influential leader in the early church. After all, he grew up as a part of that most privileged family. In James's case, however, his familiarity with Jesus was for a long time the greatest obstacle to his salvation. Like his neighbors in Nazareth, James was filled with incredulity and contempt when his older half-brother claimed to be the Messiah. His skepticism was not due to any imperfection he had seen in Jesus' character, but rather to the normality of Jesus' childhood. Perhaps James had held resentment and jealousy, probably based on the striking contrasts between him and his older sibling. Those feelings of envy became fully charged when Jesus became a popular public figure.

REACT

The Lord created, called, saved, and equipped James for usefulness in manifesting His glory. He does the same for all believers (Romans 8:29). Like James, we were all filled with contempt and hatred toward God at one time. But, if we have come to saving faith in Christ, we, too, have each been forgiven and equipped for spiritual service. Our salvation has been fully secured by grace through faith in Christ. Now, as James emphasized in his epistle, we must put feet to our faith—faithfully living in submissive obedience to the Word of God. In such living, our own story will unfold to the honor of the Lord Jesus, who is not ashamed to make us part of His family.

In what ways does your love for God affect the way you view everything else in this life?

through His eyes

What might God be able to accomplish through someone who is totally committed to honoring Him with his or her life?

TEN

MARK AND ONESIMUS:
A TALE OF TWO RUNAWAYS

HEROES BY DEFINITION are people who do not run away. They stay with courage and conviction to stand and face difficulty, accepting hardship and embracing self-sacrifice. By contrast, people who flee challenging circumstances are not viewed as heroes.

That is what makes our final two heroes so unlikely. Far from being caught in the face of a powerful enemy or dangerous circumstances, their situations were hopeful. Still they were both runaways. As He does with every sinner whom He saves, however, God pursued both Mark and Onesimus and when He caught them He turned their weaknesses and failures into strength and success.

REWIND

Scripture teaches us a couple of things about John Mark. First, it indicates that he had been raised by a devout Christian mother, whose house was a meeting place for the believers in Jerusalem. Like Timothy, who was instructed in the faith by his mother,

Eunice (2 Timothy 1:5), Mark had undoubtedly been reared in the truth by his mother, Mary. Second, the mention of Mark's name implies a direct connection between him and Peter. After being miraculously released from prison, the apostle went to the place where he knew the church gathered—namely, Mark's mother's house. The apostle's familiarity with that house, and the family who lived there, means that Peter knew Mark. As we will see, that acquaintance would prove invaluable to the young man's later life.

Evidently, Mark was not a preacher. Acts 13:1 lists the pastors and teachers in Antioch, and Mark's name is not included there. The fact that, when Paul and Barnabas left on their first missionary journey, they took Mark with them "as their assistant" (v. 5) proves he had been useful in his brief time at Antioch. They were expecting him to further assist them as they set out to preach the gospel in Asia Minor. From the start, the ministry faced difficulty.

The relentless struggles took the heart out of John Mark. Whatever the last straw, Acts 13:13 records the sad tale of his decision to abandon the mission. Evidently overwhelmed by the challenges and fearful of the outcome, Mark panicked and left, not for Antioch and the church he had been serving there, but straight back to his mother's home in Jerusalem. There was no excuse for Mark's cowardice—a fact that is confirmed in Acts 15. Several years had passed, when Paul and Barnabas decided to embark on a second missionary journey (around AD 50). As they discussed the details of their upcoming trip, Mark's abandonment came up in the planning.

Why was Mark's past behavior important to Paul and Barnabas?

How does your past affect your future usefulness for God?
How can you guard against making similar bad choices?

RETHINK

After Mark had left Paul and Barnabas behind, on that first missionary journey, he undoubtedly suffered a similar sense of shame and disgrace that would endure until he could return to the challenge of spiritual battle again. Many months later, when Paul and Barnabas came to Jerusalem and gave glowing reports of their work (Acts 15:3–4), Mark's head must have hung low in humiliation. Undoubtedly, his heart ached deeply to return and have the opportunity to be brave and faithful—to act like a man.

> Mark probably longed for an opportunity to make things right. When you have sinned against someone else, what steps should you take to make that situation right—both before the Lord and with that other person—?

What was it that changed Mark from a spiritual coward and deserter into one of Paul's most loved and honored coworkers? The answer seems to be found in Mark's friendship with the other prominent apostolic preacher—Peter. We've already noted that Peter knew Mark. And if anyone understood the shame of cowardice and the process of restoration, it was Peter. He had been restored after denying Christ three times. It turns out that it was Peter who took Mark under his wing and discipled him in the faith. What an astonishing and immense privilege Mark enjoyed—to be the companion of both Paul and Peter! As a young man, he had faltered in the field and fled in shame. But later in life he had been graciously restored to ministry usefulness and even been elevated to the sides of the two greatest apostolic preachers.

What do you think was Mark's attitude toward his responsibilities when he received a second opportunity to work alongside Paul?

To whom can you give encouragement and guidance as they seek to be useful in God's ministry?

While Mark was with Paul in Rome during the apostle's first imprisonment, he was in the company of a young man named Onesimus. Though they came from very different backgrounds, the two shared a common feature: in the past, they had both deserted their responsibility and run away. Mark had been a runaway missionary; Onesimus, a runaway slave. Yet, in God's perfect providence, both men found themselves together in Rome, in the companionship of a powerful instrument of God, the apostle Paul.

A runaway slave was a felon—guilty of a serious crime. Onesimus was a fugitive—a wanted man in the eyes of the Roman justice system. He had not only defrauded his master of his services, but likely had stolen goods or money from Philemon when he left (Philemon 18). Now that he had become a believer in Christ and been reconciled to God, Onesimus had no choice but to go back to his master and be restored as his slave.

In his letter to Philemon, Paul explained that it was a great personal sacrifice for him to send Onesimus back to Colossae. But the potential ramifications were actually much greater for Onesimus. Under Roman law, a master could punish a runaway slave in almost any way he wanted—including putting him to death. In some cases, captured runaways were branded with an *F* for "Fugitive" on their foreheads, or severely beaten for their actions. Because slaves were expensive and valuable and because the Romans were always wary of the possibility of a slave uprising, they often dealt harshly with rebels and runaways.

Onesimus had to do the right thing, even if it was painful. When have you been in a similar situation? How did you handle it?

REFLECT

The implication of Paul's letter, supported by the testimony of church history, is that Philemon responded exactly as Paul expected he would. According to the old tradition, after they reconciled, Philemon sent Onesimus back to Paul, where he continued to serve and minister to the apostle.

When we compare the lives of Mark and Onesimus we see a number of striking similarities.

- Mark was the son of a Christian woman in Jerusalem. Onesimus was the slave of a Christian family in Colossae.
- Mark ran away from the mission field in order to go back home. Onesimus ran away from home to go to a place where he became part of the mission field.
- Mark was restored to ministry and comforted Paul during the apostle's first Roman imprisonment. Onesimus was converted by Paul during that same imprisonment. and he also ministered to the apostle.
- Mark is mentioned by Paul in Colossians 4:10. Onesimus is mentioned in Colossians 4:9, just one verse earlier. Obviously Mark and Onesimus were together with Paul in Rome.
- According to church tradition, after Peter and Paul died, Mark went on to become the pastor of the church in Alexandria. Onesimus went on to become the pastor of Ephesus. Eventually, both were martyred for their unwavering faith in Jesus Christ.
- Under the inspiration of the Holy Spirit, Mark collected and preserved the preaching of Peter by writing Peter's memoirs in his gospel account. Under the providential direction of the Spirit, Onesimus helped to collect and preserve the teachings of Paul by gathering Paul's letters into one place to help form the New Testament.

Review the similarities between Mark and Onesimus. In what ways are you similar to these two men?

How do their stories affect your attitude toward your present circumstances?

REACT

The impact of these men is incalculable. Only God can comprehend their usefulness to the souls of multiplied millions through all history. We began this chapter by observing that heroes by definition are people who do not run away. That may be true. But, as we have seen with Mark and Onesimus, God is in the business of transforming defectors from weak vessels into powerful agents of His revelation and salvation. For Mark, the restored deserter, and Onesimus, the forgiven fugitive, the stories of their lives point clearly to the One who rescued them, refusing to let them go even when they tried to run away. What joy there is for us as believers—to know that in spite of all our failings, we can never outrun God's grace or His plan to use us far beyond what we could ask or imagine.

What do the testimonies of Mark and Onesimus teach us about the grace and mercy of God?

How has God revealed His grace to you?

LEADER'S GUIDE

ONE

ENOCH: THE MAN WHO WALKED WITH GOD

R EAD CHAPTER I OF *TWELVE UNLIKELY HEROES* and complete the activities in chapter 1 of the Study Guide.

REWIND

- Using your notes from reading chapter 1, recount the story of Enoch highlighting specific details relevant to your group. Ask the following question: *What spiritual characteristics come to mind when you hear the phrase "uncompromising obedience"?* Call for responses.
- Point out the significance of Enoch's character and ask group members to identify some desirable character traits. List responses on the board.
- Ask: *If only a few sentences were used to describe your character, what would be said?* Discuss responses.

RETHINK

Enoch's world looked very different than ours does today. But the culture in which he lived was the same—characterized by comprehensive corruption, moral decay in every way possible, and open rebellion against God.

- Point out the fact that people lived a long time in Enoch's day. Ask: *Based on your present rate and direction of spiritual development, would it be a blessing or a curse to live a long time? Why?*
- Arrange the group in small groups and instruct them to discuss the following questions: *What impact do you want to have on future generations? What steps are you taking right now to develop the kind of character that will outlive you?* After a few moments, call for groups to summarize their discussions.
- The Bible says Enoch walked with God. Discuss the meaning of that statement and ask: *Will a similar statement be made about you? Why or why not?*

REFLECT

In order for sinful people to commune with a holy God, they must first be reconciled to Him from their alienated sinful condition. Enoch was a man who understood his own unworthiness and the need for a proper sacrifice. Enoch understood that he was an undeserving sinner who needed a God-ordained substitute to bear the punishment in his place.

- In advance, enlist 2–3 group members to briefly share their personal stories of the beginning of their walk with God.
- Read Ephesians 1:3. Ask: *What are the blessings God provides in conjunction with our salvation experience?*
- Draw on the board a horizontal line with arrows on each end. Write "God" above the arrow to the right. Explain that God is leading us in one direction, according to the truth He has revealed in His Word. Ask: *How does God's Word provide direction for your life?*
- One of the primary evidences of genuine salvation is a sincere desire on the part of the converted to know God intimately and obey Him fully. Ask: *How does your everyday life reflect the reality of your relationship with God?* Discuss responses.
- Call on a few volunteers to share their responses to the following question: *What is your daily routine for growing in your knowledge and understanding of God and His Word?*

REACT

Though we might not escape death in this life (unless we are alive when the Lord calls the church at the Rapture), we possess the same hope Enoch had. As those who have put our faith in Jesus Christ, walking with Him in full forgiveness and intimate fellowship, we can rest assured that we have received eternal life.

- Arrange the group in smaller groups of 2–3 people and encourage them to discuss their responses to the following questions found at the end of chapter 1 in the Study Guide:

– Review Enoch's life. How does your relationship with God compare to his?
– What can you do this week to deepen your walk with the Lord?
– What priorities need to be rearranged so you can better focus on your daily walk with God?

Close the session with a time of prayer.

TWO

JOSEPH: BECAUSE GOD MEANT IT FOR GOOD

R EAD CHAPTER 2 OF *TWELVE UNLIKELY HEROES* and complete the activities in chapter 2 of the Study Guide.

REWIND

- Using your notes from reading chapter 2, recount the story of Joseph, highlighting specific details relevant to your group. Ask the following question: *Why is it hard to see bad situations as ultimately being beneficial to yourself and others?* Call for responses.
- Review some of the promises God made to Joseph and his ancestors. Ask: *Why did Joseph keep believing God would fulfill His promises?* Discuss responses.
- Ask: *What opportunities do you have because of the lessons you've learned through the struggles you have faced?* Discuss responses.

RETHINK

The environment in which Joseph grew up was filled with family tension and strife. Conflict ran in the family. There was a great deal of dysfunction in each generation.

- *Call for volunteers to describe their family relationships and some of the lessons they have learned through them.* Arrange the group in small groups and instruct them to discuss the following questions: *How does your past affect your ability to serve and honor God? Does it hinder your service or does it give you a platform from which to encourage others?* After a few moments, call for groups to summarize their discussions.
- Read aloud Genesis 37:6–8 and ask: *How would you respond to a similar message from a close relative?* Discuss responses.
- Review the low points of Joseph's story and ask: *How is it possible for you to maintain hope in the midst of circumstances you do not understand?* Discuss responses.

REFLECT

The fact that Joseph was merely thrown in jail may indicate that even though Potiphar was angry, he knew Joseph's character and was not fully convinced of his wife's credibility.

- Ask: *What steps are some things we can do to protect our character?* List responses on the board.
- God's plan for Joseph came together in God's time. Call for volunteers to describe how situations they initially did

not understand played a part in their understanding of God's plan.

- Ask: *If you had been in Joseph's situation, would you have maintained your confidence in God's plan? Why or why not?* Discuss responses.
- In a day, Joseph's fortunes had been completely reversed. That morning, he had awakened in his prison cell. By evening, he went to sleep in the palace. Ask: *How had Joseph's past experiences prepared him for his future role in the palace? What does his story teach us about the character and wisdom of God?*
- Call for volunteers to describe their daily routines for growing in their knowledge and understanding of God and His Word. Encourage group members to make their spiritual growth a priority in their daily lives.

REACT

Joseph's foresight and careful planning saved the lives of millions of people throughout the world. In an ironic turn of divine providence, Joseph's brothers came to Egypt in order to avoid death and were rescued by the very person they had sought to kill two decades earlier. Joseph was not interested in petty revenge. His trust in God's providential power outweighed any feelings of personal animosity toward his brothers. He recognized that everything that had happened to him was part of the Lord's perfect plan.

- Arrange the group in smaller groups of 2–3 people and encourage them to discuss their responses to the following questions found at the end of chapter 2 in the Study Guide:

– How did Joseph overcome his anger toward his brothers? What made it possible for him to forgive them?
– Who in your life do you need to forgive? What keeps you from offering forgiveness?

Close the session with a time of prayer.

THREE

MIRIAM: THE LEADING LADY OF THE EXODUS

R EAD CHAPTER 3 OF *TWELVE UNLIKELY HEROES* and complete the activities in chapter 3 of the Study Guide.

REWIND

- Using your notes from reading chapter 3, recount the story of Miriam, highlighting specific details relevant to your group. Ask the following question: *Why was Miriam willing to risk her life to save her brother Moses?* Call for responses.
- Talk about Miriam's bravery in light of the danger posed by the Egyptian threat. Explain that she was willing to be inconvenienced for the sake of doing something she knew was right. Ask: *What would you be willing to protect even if it meant great personal sacrifice?* Discuss responses.

RETHINK

Miriam had heard the prayers of her father, observed the affection of her mother toward Moses, and witnessed the faith of both in their protective defiance of Pharaoh's edict.

- Explain that Miriam connected the prayers of her parents with her role in the story. Arrange the group in small groups and instruct them to discuss the following question: *Who are some examples of steadfast faith in your life? What have you learned by watching them?* After a few moments, call for groups to summarize their discussions.
- Ask: *What might have happened if Miriam had been unwilling to play an active part in protecting her brother?* Discuss responses.
- Remind learners that Miriam never envisioned everything that happened; she simply was willing to do what was right at the moment she had the opportunity. Ask: *How do you know what's right?* Call for responses, then follow up by asking: *How willing are you to take action when given the opportunity?* Discuss responses.
- Gather information about the preschool, children's, and student ministries at your church. Highlight the value of those ministries and then ask: *Why is it so important for parents to take the lead in teaching their children about God?* Discuss responses.
- Ask: *What might have happened in Miriam's life if her parents had left her spiritual development to others?* Spend a few moments discussing responses.

REFLECT

After he committed murder, Moses fled to Midian—the place where he would spend the next four decades of his life tending sheep and being humbled and shaped by God.

- Ask: *What did God teach Moses through his forty years of exile? Have you ever experienced a time of significant transition or extended hardship? What did God teach you through that situation?* Allow time for a few volunteers to respond.
- Miriam remained in Egypt and waited forty years for a deliverer. Ask: *Would you have held on to hope for that long? Why or why not?* Discuss responses.
- Moses eventually returned to lead the Israelites to freedom. Ask: *In what ways is Israel's deliverance from Egypt a fitting picture of salvation from sin?* Discuss responses.
- The mood of the Hebrews was dampened when they saw the Egyptian army approaching. Quickly their jubilation turned into complaints. They allowed their immediate circumstances to cloud their trust in God's power and deliverance. Ask: *What situations in our lives can tempt us to doubt God's promises?* Call for volunteers to respond.

REACT

As the Hebrew people crossed the Red Sea on dry land, Miriam must have felt a sense of awe. It was the brother she helped save who led the way. As they reached the other side, the people watched in amazement as the walls of water crashed together with a violence never occurring in any ordinary sea. In one catastrophic holocaust, the waters returned to their normal level to bury the mighty and massive army of Egypt like drowned rats.

- Read Exodus 15:20–21. Ask: *What does this passage teach about Miriam's character and her relationship with God?* Call for responses.
- Arrange the group in smaller groups of 2–3 people and encourage them to discuss their responses to the following question found at the end of chapter 3 in the Study Guide:

  – *What are you doing now to create a lasting legacy of faithfulness to God?*

Close the session with a time of prayer.

FOUR

GIDEON AND SAMSON: STORIES OF WEAKNESS AND STRENGTH

R EAD CHAPTER 4 OF *TWELVE UNLIKELY HEROES* and complete the activities in chapter 4 of the Study Guide.

REWIND

- Using your notes from reading chapter 4, describe the role of judges in the history of Israel. Ask the following questions: *Why did God allow the Israelites' enemies to oppress them? Why did He later respond by raising up a human deliverer to rescue them?* Call for responses.
- Explain that the book of Judges is a record of Israel's repeated disobedience. Ask: *When we persist in sinful disobedience, what should we expect from the Lord? How will He respond to us when we repent and ask for His forgiveness?* Discuss responses.

RETHINK

When we first meet Gideon, he is hiding from the Midianites—attempting to covertly thresh wheat in a winepress (Judges 6:11).

- Remind learners that although people today don't face the threat of a Midianite invasion, many still live in fear and apprehension. Ask: *What things tempt you to become fearful and to stop trusting the Lord?* Call for responses. Call for volunteers to explain the fears that caused them to try to hide from God.
- Gideon listened to the word of the Lord and was willing to obey, even though he was still fearful. Ask: *What are some biblical commands that Christians find hard to obey due to their own apprehensions?* Discuss responses.
- Arrange learners in small groups and instruct them to discuss some practical ways in which they can overcome those fears. After a few moments, call for groups to share summaries of their discussions.
- Remind learners that God often reveals His strength through our weaknesses. Ask: *In what areas of your life is God working to show His might?* Discuss responses.

REFLECT

Though Samson began with power and confidence, his end was tragic. The closing drama of his life features a man who completely failed to advance from the reckless impulsiveness of his youth.

- Ask: *What habits in your life might negatively affect your usefulness to God?* Allow time for a few volunteers to respond.
- Highlight some examples of Samson's arrogance. Ask: *How did Samson's arrogance open the door to his ultimate failure?* Discuss responses.
- Samson eventually succumbed to his moral frailty. Ask: *What do you think was the turning point in Samson's story?* Discuss responses.
- Discuss the importance of protecting oneself morally. Ask: *What steps should believers take to protect themselves from moral failure?* Call for responses.

REACT

Both of these men are presented as examples of faith in the New Testament. Their legacies might best be summarized by the phrase in Hebrews 11:34, "out of weakness [they] were made strong." It was in their moments of greatest frailty, when they were most dependent on the Lord through faith, that they were the strongest, because that was when God's power was displayed through them. Their heroism in the redemptive purposes of God was inseparably tied to their humiliation.

- Read 2 Corinthians 12:8–10. Ask: *How does this passage relate to your everyday life?* Call for responses.
- Arrange the group in smaller groups of 2–3 people and encourage them to discuss their responses to the following question found at the end of chapter 4 in the Study Guide:

– What might God do through your life when it is completely submitted to Him and His Word? Call for responses.

Close the session with a time of prayer.

FIVE

JONATHAN: THE MAN WHO WOULD (NOT) BE KING

READ CHAPTER 5 OF *TWELVE UNLIKELY HEROES* and complete the activities in chapter 5 of the Study Guide.

REWIND

- Using your notes from reading chapter 5, describe the spiritual significance of Israel's desire for a human king. Point out the characteristics of a king and ask the following question: *What opportunities do you have to demonstrate your character and confidence in God?* Call for responses.
- Explain that kings were human, therefore they had weaknesses that could cause them problems. Ask: *What weaknesses do you have that might hinder your ability to be a spiritual leader? What are you doing to overcome those weaknesses?* Discuss responses.

RETHINK

Saul's disobedience to God eventually cost him his opportunity to lead. Saul tried to explain away his sin. Saul employed a familiar, time-honored, "blame-someone-else" strategy. Like everyone else, he experienced disastrous results.

- Saul refused to take the blame for his actions and placed the blame on others. Ask: *How do you feel when you are blamed for something you did not do?* Discuss responses.
- Ask: *Why is it sometimes hard to take responsibility for our sin?* List responses on the board. Ask: *Which of these excuses do you see evidenced in Saul's life?* Circle words or phrases as they are suggested.
- Arrange learners in small groups and instruct them to consider some of the information they learned about Jonathan. After a few moments, instruct groups to discuss these questions: *When there is a spiritual battle, are you more like Jonathan or Saul? What victories has God brought into your life? Where should you place your hope and faith when you face challenging circumstances?* After a few moments, call for volunteers to share summaries of their discussions.
- Saul eventually started thinking more and more irrationally. He even ordered that his son, Jonathan, be put to death for violating an irrational oath. Ask: *What caused Saul to behave so irrationally?* Discuss responses. Then ask: *What does Saul's behavior say about his relationship with God?* Allow time for discussion.

REFLECT

By failing to trust the Lord and by offering sacrifices before Samuel arrived, Saul proved to be an incompetent leader who left behind a royal mess.

- Point out that Saul's example teaches us that incomplete obedience to the Word of God is really disobedience. Ask: *In what ways are you tempted not to obey God's Word completely?* Allow time for a few volunteers to respond.
- Remind learners that we all have a spiritual existence and a physical existence and that God sees the heart, not the external person. Ask: *Are you working more on developing your physical attributes or your spiritual attributes? What is your workout regimen for spiritual development?* Discuss responses.

REACT

Jonathan's character is evidenced most clearly in his attitude toward David. Without question, he was a mighty warrior, a noble prince, and a loyal friend. But it was his unwavering faith in the Lord's plan for him and his future that set him apart as an unlikely hero. Jonathan did not merely *accept* his non-kingly role; he *embraced* it wholeheartedly—eagerly protecting and promoting the one whom God had appointed to be king instead of him.

- Ask: *How are you responding to your current circumstances and the position in life where God has placed you?* Call for responses.

- Arrange the group in smaller groups of 2–3 people and encourage them to discuss their responses to the following question found at the end of chapter 5 in the Study Guide:

  – *In what ways are you supporting others who are engaged in serving God? Call for responses.*

Close the session with a time of prayer.

SIX

JONAH: THE WORLD'S GREATEST FISH STORY

R EAD CHAPTER 6 OF *TWELVE UNLIKELY HEROES* and complete the activities in chapter 6 of the Study Guide.

REWIND

- Using your notes from reading chapter 6, describe Jonah's initial instructions from God. Point out Jonah's hasty disobedience and ask: *What happens when believers run away from God in disobedience?* Call for responses.
- Explain that Jonah's disobedience affected him, the Ninevites, and the sailors on the boat he boarded. Ask: *In what ways does your disobedience impact those around you?* Discuss responses.

RETHINK

Jonah had his reasons for fleeing in the direction away from Nineveh. The Assyrians were a notoriously brutal and wicked people. Assyrian kings boasted of the horrific ways in which they massacred their enemies and mutilated their captives—from dismemberment to decapitation to burning prisoners alive to other indescribably gory forms of torture. They posed a clear and present danger to the national security of Israel.

- Jonah had no trouble coming up with excuses to legitimize his disobedience to God's instructions. Ask: *Have you ever excused yourself from doing something you knew God wanted you to do? How so?* Discuss responses.
- Jonah was afraid of the Ninevites, but he also wasn't willing to do something outside his comfort zone. Ask: *Was your disobedience caused more by your fear or by your desire for comfort and convenience?* Call for responses.
- Jonah's hatred toward people God loved put him in jeopardy. Ask: *How do your prejudices affect your willingness to be used by God?* Call for volunteers to share their thoughts.
- Arrange learners in small groups and instruct them to consider some of the details about Jonah's life. After a few moments, instruct groups to discuss this question: *What would you do if given an assignment similar to the one given to Jonah?* After a few moments, call for volunteers to share summaries of their discussions.
- Everything that God allowed to happen was for the purpose of bringing Jonah back into a right relationship with Him. Ask: *Have you ever resisted repenting for a sin you committed against God?* Discuss responses. Then ask:

Why were you determined not to repent? Allow time for discussion.

REFLECT

Jonah's three-day stay inside a fish was an indescribable horror. Lodged in the cramped and clammy darkness, he was likely unable to move and barely able to breathe due to the suffocating stench. The gastric acids of the fish's stomach ate away at his skin, and the constant motion of the fish combined with the changing pressure of the ocean's depths must have been absolutely nauseating. In the midst of his misery, the humbled prophet cried out for deliverance.

- Arrange learners in small groups and instruct them to read Jonah 2 and to discuss times when they cried out to God. After several moments, call for volunteers to share their thoughts.
- Jonah's experience in the fish changed his heart. Ask: *In what ways was God's mercy demonstrated toward Jonah in giving him a second opportunity to obey? Are there areas in your life where obedience is needed?* Discuss responses.

REACT

Jonah recognized the magnitude of God's grace, which is why he initially ran in the opposite direction; he wanted nothing to do with divine pardon being extended to Israel's hostile enemies. Ironically, when Jonah himself was in trouble, he cried out for God's mercy. But when the Lord extended grace to others, Jonah was filled with resentment. When God's wrath was withheld from the Ninevites, the prophet's wrath was aroused.

- Ask: *What in this story relates most closely to your life?* Call for responses.
- Arrange the group in smaller groups of 2–3 people and encourage them to discuss their responses to the following questions found at the end of chapter 6 in the Study Guide:

  – *Jonah did what was right with a bad attitude. Describe a time when you have done the same thing. What do you think God's assessment of wrong motives is? Discuss responses.*
  – *Why was your attitude bad? What did God teach you through that experience? Call for responses.*

Close the session with a time of prayer.

SEVEN

ESTHER: FOR SUCH A TIME AS THIS

R EAD CHAPTER 7 OF *TWELVE UNLIKELY HEROES* and complete the activities in chapter 7 of the Study Guide.

REWIND

- Using your notes from reading chapter 7, briefly describe the relationship between Esther and Mordecai. Point out the fact that they were Jews living in the Persian Empire and ask: *Why was it hard for Jewish people to live in the Persian Empire?* Call for responses.
- Explain that Mordecai had a strong relationship with God. Ask: *Based on what you read about Mordecai, which of his character traits stand out?* List responses on the board.

RETHINK

An obscure Jewish orphan girl was exalted to the highest position of any woman in the world at that time. Out of the twenty-five million women in the empire, it had come down to Esther being singled out by the king himself. This was clearly no coincidence. A Power infinitely greater than Ahasuerus was at work, providentially orchestrating His purposes through the emperor's affections.

- Ask: *What would you do if you overheard a plot similar to the plot Mordecai overheard?* Discuss responses.
- Remind learners that Mordecai was a Jew. Ask: *Why did he report the assassination plot against the Persian king?* Call for responses.
- Discuss the king's journal and the kinds of information it contained about acts of valor and service. Ask: *What would God write in His record book regarding your loyalty to Him?* Discuss responses.
- Follow up by asking: *Would an assessment of your loyalty and faithfulness to the Lord be cause for celebration or punishment?* Call for volunteers to respond.

REFLECT

Haman sought the advice of Persian magicians and astrologers who cast lots to determine the optimum day on which to annihilate the Jewish people. He then went to the king and deceitfully misrepresented the Jews as a rebellious threat to the empire who needed to be eliminated. Haman proposed that all Jews living within the Persian Empire ought to be killed.

- Arrange learners in small groups and instruct them to discuss Haman's plot. Explain that Haman's plot was his way to manipulate a situation to gain favor and to seek revenge. After several moments, ask: *In what ways are people today tempted to do something similar to what Haman did?* Call for responses.
- Ask: *How can Christians avoid the trap of that kind of deceptive scheming against others?* Discuss responses.
- Point out that Esther was willing to put her life on the line in order to save the Jewish people. Ask: *For whom or what would you put your life on the line?* Discuss responses.
- If time allows, ask: *How does your love for God influence your recognition of those things for which you are willing to fight? Are the things you are willing to fight for important to God? How do you know? What can you do to develop a biblical set of priorities?* Discuss responses.

REACT

The book of Esther might be compared to a chess match, in which God and Satan—working behind the scenes—moved real-life kings, queens, and nobles. It looked as though Satan, using Haman, might put God's plans in check. But the Lord—who has absolute power over Satan—checkmated the devil's schemes by positioning Mordecai and Esther to find favor with the king.

- In spite of her upbringing, Esther became a powerful instrument in the hand of God. Ask: *What does that teach us about the power and purposes of God? Are there any limitations that He cannot overcome?* Call for responses.

- Arrange the group in smaller groups of 2–3 people and encourage them to discuss their responses to the following question found at the end of chapter 7 in the Study Guide:

  – Read Romans 8:28–29. In what ways does the power of God, as described in that passage, encourage your heart? Discuss responses.

Close the session with a time of prayer.

EIGHT

JOHN THE BAPTIST: THE TRUE MEANING OF GREATNESS

R EAD CHAPTER 8 OF *TWELVE UNLIKELY HEROES* and complete the activities in chapter 8 of the Study Guide.

REWIND

- Using your notes from reading chapter 8, briefly describe the genealogy of John the Baptist. Point out the fact that the Jews were anticipating a Messiah and John's arrival was consistent with Old Testament prophecy. Ask: *What was John the Baptist's message? Why was it needed after four hundred silent years?* Call for responses.
- John's role was to point people to the Lord Jesus Christ. Ask: *Why is that message still needed today?* Call for responses.

RETHINK

Like the Old Testament prophets before him, everything about John's strange behavior was intended as an object lesson for God's chosen nation. He was not calling others to live or dress as he did; but he was calling people away from liturgically dressed hypocrites who were leading people to hell.

- Ask: *In what ways are you called to announce Jesus to the world?* Discuss responses.
- Call for volunteers to identify characteristics of messages or advertisements they find believable. List responses on the board. Ask: *What about your walk with God makes your message about Him believable? Are you a credible witness? Why or why not?* Call for responses.
- John's message shocked the Jewish people because they assumed they were already included because they belonged to God's chosen nation. By ethnicity, they felt assured of a place in the kingdom of heaven, so that repentance was not necessary for them. Ask: *In what ways do people today reflect the entitlement attitude of the Jews regarding their place in heaven?* Discuss responses.
- Follow up by asking: *If someone told you he or she deserved to go to heaven, how would you respond? How would verses like Romans 3:23 and 6:23 affect your answer?* Call for volunteers to respond.
- Explain that John knew his responsibility and his task. Ask: *What are some practical ways that you can tell others about Jesus?* Call for responses. Then arrange learners in small groups and encourage them to develop a list of ways people today can make God known to the world. After a few moments, summarize the list on the board. Ask: *What are*

steps you are going to take to initiate conversations about the good news of salvation with the people in your life? Discuss responses.

REFLECT

John's baptism was a way for sinners to physically symbolize their repentance from sin. But Jesus came to be baptized even though He was absolutely sinless. Bewildered, John must have wondered, *Why would the perfect One who takes away the sins of the world want to participate in a ceremony that symbolizes a turning from sin?*

- Ask: *Why was John so reluctant to baptize Jesus?* Discuss responses.
- Arrange learners in small groups and instruct them to turn to page 62 in the study guide and to discuss their responses to the three things Jesus' baptism revealed about his character and purpose. After a few moments, call for groups to report their findings.

REACT

It may be a shock to our superficial society to learn that true greatness is not defined in terms of human achievement, athletic prowess, financial gain, political power, or celebrity status. Instead, it is measured by how one relates to the person and work of Jesus Christ. John the Baptist was great because of his proximity to the Messiah. Similarly for us, true greatness is found in faithfully acknowledging the Savior. It is derived from our relationship to the One far greater than John—the Lord Jesus Christ.

- Ask: *What is your definition of greatness? How does it compare to the greatness demonstrated by John?* Call for responses.
- Arrange the group in smaller groups of 2–3 people and encourage them to discuss their responses to the following question found at the end of chapter 8 in the Study Guide:

  – *What are you doing in your life to become great in God's eyes? What priorities need to change (see 1 Peter 5:5–6)?* Discuss responses.

Close the session with a time of prayer.

NINE

James: The Brother of Our Lord

R EAD CHAPTER 9 OF *TWELVE UNLIKELY HEROES* and complete the activities in chapter 9 of the Study Guide.

REWIND

- Using your notes from reading chapter 9, briefly describe what it might have been like to grow up in Jesus' family. Ask: *Why was it hard for Jesus' siblings to believe He was the Messiah?* Call for responses.
- Explain that Jesus' siblings eventually came to believe in Him. Ask: *What do you think happened that made Jesus' siblings believe in Him?* Call for responses. Then ask: *What happened in your life to cause you to believe in Jesus?* Allow volunteers to respond.

RETHINK

Although James had known Jesus for more than three decades, he did not believe in Him until his risen brother graciously appeared to him and saved him. At the establishment of the church, James was poised for usefulness in ministry.

- Explain that God equips us to carry out the ministry He assigns to us. Ask: *How has God uniquely gifted you? In what ways are your gifts being used for His glory and honor?* Call for responses.
- James was effective in ministry and left a legacy for future generations. Ask: *What will be your spiritual legacy?* Discuss responses.
- Follow up by asking: *In what ways are you making a positive impact for the sake of the Lord Jesus on your church and community?* Call for volunteers to respond.

REFLECT

Review the five things that stand out about James (pp.68–69 in the Study Guide). Arrange learners in groups and instruct them to discuss the five things that made James unique. After a few moments, ask and discuss responses to the following questions:

- *What might people say about your humility?*
- *What might people say about your righteousness?*
- *What might people say about your self-sacrifice in ministry?*
- *What might people say about your personal spiritual disciplines?*

- *What might people say about your knowledge of God's Word?*
- *In which areas are you the strongest?*
- *In which areas are you the weakest? What is your plan for improving these areas?*

REACT

Like James, we were all filled with contempt and hatred toward God at one time. But if we have come to saving faith in Christ, we, too, have each been forgiven and equipped for spiritual service. Our salvation has been fully secured by grace through faith in Christ. Now, as James emphasized in his epistle, we must put feet to our faith—faithfully living in submissive obedience to the Word of God. In such living, our own story will unfold to the honor of the Lord Jesus, who is not ashamed to make us part of His family.

- Arrange the group in smaller groups of 2–3 people and encourage them to discuss their responses to the following questions found at the end of chapter 9 in the Study Guide:

  - *In what ways does your love for God affect the way you view everything else in life?* Discuss responses.
  - *What might God be able to accomplish through someone who is totally committed to honoring Him with his or her life?* Discuss responses.

Close the session with a time of prayer.

TEN

MARK AND ONESIMUS:
A TALE OF TWO RUNAWAYS

READ CHAPTER 10 OF *TWELVE UNLIKELY HEROES* and complete the activities in chapter 10 of the Study Guide.

REWIND

- Using your notes from reading chapter 10, briefly describe the situations that set the context for the stories of Mark and Onesimus. Ask: *Why was Mark's past behavior important to Paul and Barnabas?* Call for responses.
- Explain that our experiences either prepare us for ministry or interfere with our ability to minister. Ask: *How does your past affect your future usefulness for God? How can you guard against making similar bad choices?* Call for volunteers to respond.

RETHINK

After Mark had left Paul and Barnabas behind on that first missionary journey, he undoubtedly suffered a similar sense of shame and disgrace that would endure until he could return to the challenge of spiritual battle again. Many months later, when Paul and Barnabas came to Jerusalem and gave glowing reports of their work (Acts 15:3–4), Mark's head must have hung low in humiliation. Undoubtedly, his heart ached deeply to return and have the opportunity to be brave and faithful—to act like a man.

- Explain that Mark's defection had prolonged consequences. Ask: *When you have sinned against someone else, what steps should you take to make that situation right—both before the Lord and with the other person?* Discuss responses.
- Mark eventually received a second opportunity. Ask: *What do you think was Mark's attitude toward his responsibilities when he received a second opportunity to work alongside Paul?* Call for responses.
- Follow up by asking: *To whom can you give encouragement and guidance as they seek to be useful in God's ministry?* Call for volunteers to respond.
- Recount the story of Onesimus and point out that he had to do the right thing even if it was painful. Ask: *When have you been in a similar situation? How did you handle it?* Call for responses.

REFLECT

Use the information on page 77 of the study guide to highlight the similarities between the stories of Mark and Onesimus. In summary:

1. Mark was the son of a Christian woman in Jerusalem. Onesimus was the slave of a Christian family in Colossae.

2. Mark ran away from the mission field in order to go back home. Onesimus ran away from home to go to a place where he became part of the mission field.

3. Mark was restored to ministry and comforted Paul during the apostle's first Roman imprisonment. Onesimus was converted by Paul during that same imprisonment, and he also ministered to the apostle.

4. Mark is mentioned by Paul in Colossians 4:10. Onesimus is mentioned in Colossians 4:9, just one verse earlier. Obviously Mark and Onesimus were together with Paul in Rome.

5. According to church tradition, after Peter and Paul died, Mark went on to become the pastor of the church in Alexandria. Onesimus went on to become the pastor of Ephesus. Eventually, both were martyred for their unwavering faith in Jesus Christ.

6. Under the inspiration of the Holy Spirit, Mark collected and preserved the preaching of Peter by writing Peter's memoirs in his gospel account. Under the providential direction of the Spirit, Onesimus helped to collect and preserve the teachings of Paul by gathering Paul's letters into one place to help form the New Testament.

- Arrange learners in small groups and ask: *In what ways are you similar to these two men?* After a few moments, discuss responses.
- Then ask: *How do their stories affect your attitude toward your present circumstances?* Discuss responses.

REACT

The impact of these men is incalculable. Only God can comprehend their usefulness to the souls of multiplied millions through all history. We began this chapter by observing that heroes by definition are people who do not run away. That may be true. But, as we have seen with Mark and Onesimus, God is in the business of transforming defectors from weak vessels into powerful agents of His revelation and salvation. For Mark, the restored deserter, and Onesimus, the forgiven fugitive, the stories of their lives point clearly to the One who rescued them, refusing to let them go even when they tried to run away. What joy there is for us as believers—to know that in spite of all of our failings, we can never outrun God's grace or His plan to use us far beyond what we could ask or imagine.

- Arrange the group in smaller groups of 2-3 people and encourage them to discuss their responses to the following questions found at the end of chapter 10 in the Study Guide:

  - *What do the testimonies of Mark and Onesimus teach us about the grace and mercy of God?*
  - *How has God revealed His grace to you?*

Close the session with a time of prayer.

THE TRUTH ABOUT SERIES

THE TRUTH ABOUT . . . Grace

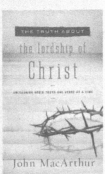

THE TRUTH ABOUT . . . The Lordship of Christ

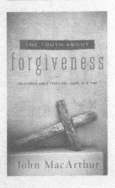

THE TRUTH ABOUT . . . Forgiveness

Available wherever books and ebooks are sold.